Building Isomorphic JavaScript Apps

From Concept to Implementation to
Real-World Solutions

Jason Strimpel and Maxime Najim

Beijing · Boston · Farnham · Sebastopol · Tokyo

Building Isomorphic JavaScript Apps

by Jason Strimpel and Maxime Najim

Printed in the United States of America.

Published by O'Reilly Media, Inc., 1005 Gravenstein Highway North, Sebastopol, CA 95472.

O'Reilly books may be purchased for educational, business, or sales promotional use. Online editions are also available for most titles (*http://safaribooksonline.com*). For more information, contact our corporate/institutional sales department: 800-998-9938 or *corporate@oreilly.com*.

Editor: Allyson MacDonald	**Indexer:** WordCo Indexing Services, Inc.
Production Editor: Nicholas Adams	**Interior Designer:** David Futato
Copyeditor: Rachel Head	**Cover Designer:** Randy Comer
Proofreader: Colleen Toporek	**Illustrator:** Rebecca Demarest

September 2016: First Edition

Revision History for the First Edition
2016-09-08: First Release

See *http://oreilly.com/catalog/errata.csp?isbn=9781491932933* for release details.

978-1-491-93293-3

[LSI]

Table of Contents

Part III.   Real-World Solutions

Preface

Jason Strimpel

I began my web development career many years ago, when I was hired as an administrative assistant at the University of California, San Diego. One of my job duties was to maintain the department website. It was the time of webmasters, table-based layouts, and CGI-BIN(s), and Netscape Navigator was still a major player in the browser market. As for my level of technical expertise, I think the following anecdote paints a clearer picture of my inexperience than Bob Ross's desire for a happy little tree. I can clearly remember being concerned that if I sent an email with misspellings, the recipient would see my mistakes underlined in red the same way I saw them. Fortunately, I had a patient supervisor who assured me this was not the case and then handed me the keys to the website!

Fast-forward 15 years, and now I am an industry "expert" speaking at conferences, managing open source projects, coauthoring books, etc. I ask myself, "Well... How did I get here?" The answer to that question is not by letting the days go by—at least, not entirely so.

Why Isomorphic JavaScript

The latest chapter in my web journey is working on the Platform team at WalmartLabs, and it is here that my adventures in isomorphic JavaScript began. When I started at WalmartLabs I was placed on a team that was tasked with creating a new web framework from scratch that could power large, public-facing websites. In addition to meeting the minimum requirements for a public-facing website, SEO support, and an optimized page load, it was important to our team to keep UI engineers—myself included—happy and productive. The obvious choice for appeasing UI engineers would have been to extend an existing single-page application (*http://en.wikipedia.org/wiki/Single-page_application*) (SPA) solution. The problem with the SPA model is that it doesn't support the minimum requirements out of the box (see "The Perfect Storm: An All-Too-Common Story" on page xi and "Single-page web application" on page 9 for more details)—so we decided to take the isomorphic path. Here is why:

- It uses a single code base for the UI with a common rendering lifecycle. This means no duplication of efforts, which reduces the UI development and maintenance cost, allowing teams to ship features faster.

- It renders the initial response HTML on the server for a faster perceived page load, because the user doesn't have to wait for the application to bootstrap and fetch data before the page is rendered in the browser. The improved perceived page load is even more important in areas with high network latency.

- It supports SEO because it uses qualified URLs (no fragments) and gracefully degrades to server rendering (for subsequent page requests) for clients that don't support the History API.

- It uses distributed rendering of the SPA model for subsequent page requests for clients that support the History API, which lessens application server loads.

- It gives UI engineers full control of the UI (*http://bit.ly/nodejsweb*), be it on the server or the client, and provides clear lines of separation between the back- and frontends, which helps reduce operating costs.

Those are the primary reasons our team went down the isomorphic JavaScript path. Before we get into the details of isomorphic JavaScript, though, it is good idea to provide some background about the environment in which we find ourselves today.

The Evolution of a Platform

It is hard to imagine, but the Web of today did not always exist. It did not always have JavaScript or CSS, either. They were introduced to browsers to provide an interaction model and a separation of concerns. Remember the numerous articles advocating the separation of structure, style, and behavior? Even with the addition of these technologies, the architecture of applications changed very little. A document was requested using a URI, parsed by the browser, and rendered. The only difference was the UI was a bit richer thanks to JavaScript. Then Microsoft introduced a technology that would be the catalyst for transforming the Web into an application platform: XMLHttpRequest (*https://developer.mozilla.org/en-US/docs/Web/API/XMLHttpRequest*).

Ajax: Rise of an Application Platform

As much disdain as frontend engineers have for Microsoft and Internet Explorer, they should also harbor an even greater sense of gratitude. If it weren't for Microsoft, frontend engineers would likely have much less fulfilling careers. Without the advent of XMLHttpRequest there would not be Ajax; without Ajax we wouldn't have such a great need to modify documents; without the need to modify documents we wouldn't have the need for jQuery (*https://jquery.com/*). You see where this is going? We would not have the rich landscape of frontend MV* libraries and the single-page application pattern, which gave way to the History API. So next time you are battling Internet Explorer, make sure to balance your hatred with gratitude for Microsoft. After all, they changed the course of history and laid the groundwork that provides you with a playground in which to exercise your mind.

Ajax: Accumulation of Technical Debt

As influential as Ajax was in shaping of the web platform, it also left behind a path of destruction in the form of technical debt. Ajax blurred the lines of what had previously been a clearly defined model, where the browser requests, receives, and parses a full document response when a user navigates to a new page or submits form data. This all changed when Ajax made its way into mainstream web development. An engineer could now respond to a user's request for more data or another view without the overhead of requesting a new document from the server. This allowed an application to update regions of a page. This ability drastically optimized both the client and the server and vastly improved the user experience. Unfortunately, client application architecture was virtually nonexistent, and those tasked with working in the view layer did not have the background required to properly support this change of paradigm. These factors compounded with time and turned applications into maintenance nightmares. The lines had been blurred, and a period of painful growth was about to begin.

The Perfect Storm: An All-Too-Common Story

Imagine you are on a team that maintains the code responsible for rendering the product page for an ecommerce application. In the righthand gutter of the product page is a carousel of consumer reviews that a user can paginate through. When a user clicks on a review pagination link, the client updates the URI and makes a request to the server to fetch the product page. As an engineer, this inefficiency bothers you greatly. You shouldn't need to reload the entire page and make the data calls required to fully rerender the page. All you really need to do is GET the HTML for the next page of reviews. Fortunately you keep up on technical advances in the industry and you've recently learned of Ajax, which you have been itching to try out. You put together a proof of concept (POC) and pitch it to your manager. You look like a wizard. The POC is moved into production like all other POCs.

You are satisfied until you hear of a new data-interchange format called JSON being espoused by the unofficial spokesman of JavaScript, Douglas Crockford (*http://www.crockford.com/*). You are immediately dissatisfied with your current implementation. The next day you put together a new POC using something you read about called micro-templating (*http://ejohn.org/blog/javascript-micro-templating/*). You show the new POC to your manager. It is well-received and moved into production. You are a god among mortal engineers. Then there is a bug in the reviews code. Your manager looks to you to resolve the bug because you implemented this magic. You review the code and assure your manager that the bug is in the server-side rendering. You then get to have the joyful conversation about why there are two different rendering implementations. After you finish explaining why Java will not run in the browser, you assure your manager that the duplication was worth the cost because it greatly improved the user experience. The bug is then passed around like a hot potato until eventually it is fixed.

Despite the DRY (don't repeat yourself) violations, you are hailed as an expert. Slowly the pattern you implemented is copied throughout the code base. But as your pattern permeates the code base, the unthinkable happens. The bug count begins to rise, and developers are afraid to make code changes out of fear of causing a regression. The technical debt is now larger than the national deficit, engineering managers are getting pushback from developers, and product people are getting pushback from engineering managers. The application is brittle and the company is unable to react quickly enough to changes in the market. You feel an overwhelming sense of guilt. Luckily, you have been reading about this new pattern called single-page application…

Client Architecture to the Rescue

Recently you have been reading articles about people's frustration with the lack of architecture in the frontend. Often these people blame jQuery, even though it was only intended to be a façade for the DOM. Fortunately, others in the industry have already faced the exact problem you are facing and did not stop at the uninformed critiques of others. One of them was Jeremy Ashkenas (*https://github.com/jashkenas*), the author of Backbone (*http://backbonejs.org/*).

You take a look at Backbone and read some articles. You are sold. It separates application logic from data retrieval, consolidates UI code to a single language and runtime, and significantly reduces the impact on the servers. "Eureka!" you shout triumphantly in your head. This will solve all our problems. You put together another POC, and so it goes.

What Happened to Our Visits?

You are soon known as the savior. Your newest SPA pattern is adopted company-wide. Bug counts begin to drop and engineering confidence returns. The fear once associated with shipping code has practically vanished. Then a product person comes knocking at your door and informs you that site visits have plummeted since the SPA model was implemented. Welcome to the joys of the hash fragment hack. After some exhaustive research, you determine that search engines do not take into account to the `window.location.hash` portion of the URI that the `Backbone.Router` uses to create linkable, bookmarkable, shareable page views. So when a search engine crawls the application, there is not any content to index. Now you are in an even worse place than you were before. This is having a direct impact on sales. So you begin a cycle of research and development once again. It turns out you have two options. The first option is to spin up new servers, emulate the DOM to run your client application, and redirect search engines to these servers. The second option is to pay another company to solve the problem for you. Both options have a cost, which is in addition to the drop in revenues that the SPA implementation cost the company.

Isomorphic JavaScript: A Brave New World

The previous story was spun together from personal experience and stories that I have read or heard from other engineers. If you have ever worked on a particular web application for long enough, then I am sure you have similar stories and experiences. Some of these issues are from days of yore and some of them still exist today. Some potential issues were not even highlighted—e.g., poorly optimized page loads and perceived rendering. Consolidating the route response/rendering lifecycle to a common code base that runs on the client and server could potentially solve these problems and others. This is what isomorphic JavaScript is all about. It is about taking the best from two different architectures to create easier-to-maintain applications that provide better user experiences.

The Road Ahead

The primary goal of this book is to provide the foundational knowledge required to implement and understand existing isomorphic JavaScript solutions available in the industry today. The intent is to provide you with the information required to make an informed decision as to whether isomorphic JavaScript is a viable solution for your use case, and then allow some of the brightest minds in the industry to share their solutions so that you do not have to reinvent the wheel.

Part I provides an introduction to the subject, beginning with a detailed examination of the different kinds of web application architectures. It covers the rationale and use cases for isomorphic JavaScript, such as SEO support and improving perceived page loads. It then outlines the different types of isomorphic JavaScript applications, such as real-time and SPA-like applications. It also covers the different pieces that make up isomorphic solutions, like implementations that provide environment shims/abstractions and implementations that are truly environment agnostic. The section concludes by laying the code foundation for Part II.

Part II breaks the topic down into the key concepts that are common in most isomorphic JavaScript solutions. Each concept is implemented without the aid of existing libraries such as React (*https://facebook.github.io/react/*), Backbone (*http://backbo nejs.org/*), or Ember (*http://emberjs.com/*). This is done so that the concept is not obfuscated by a particular implementation.

In Part III, industry experts weigh in on the topic with their solutions.

Conventions Used in This Book

The following typographical conventions are used in this book:

Italic
> Indicates new terms, URLs, email addresses, filenames, and file extensions.

`Constant width`
> Used for program listings, as well as within paragraphs to refer to program elements such as variable or function names, class, data types, statements, and keywords. Also used for module and package names and for commands and command-line output.

`Constant width bold`
> Shows commands or other text that should be typed literally by the user.

`Constant width italic`
> Shows text that should be replaced with user-supplied values or by values determined by context.

 This element signifies a tip or suggestion.

 This element signifies a general note.

 This element indicates a warning or caution.

Using Code Examples

Supplemental material (code examples, exercises, etc.) is available for download at *https://github.com/isomorphic-javascript-book*.

This book is here to help you get your job done. In general, if example code is offered with this book, you may use it in your programs and documentation. You do not need to contact us for permission unless you're reproducing a significant portion of the code. For example, writing a program that uses several chunks of code from this book does not require permission. Selling or distributing a CD-ROM of examples from O'Reilly books does require permission. Answering a question by citing this book and quoting example code does not require permission. Incorporating a significant amount of example code from this book into your product's documentation does require permission.

We appreciate, but do not require, attribution. An attribution usually includes the title, author, publisher, and ISBN. For example: "*Building Isomorphic JavaScript Apps* by Jason Strimpel and Maxime Najim (O'Reilly). Copyright 2016 Jason Strimpel and Maxime Najim, 978-1-491-93293-3."

If you feel your use of code examples falls outside fair use or the permission given above, feel free to contact us at *permissions@oreilly.com*.

Safari® Books Online

 *Safari Books Online* is an on-demand digital library that delivers expert content in both book and video form from the world's leading authors in technology and business.

Technology professionals, software developers, web designers, and business and creative professionals use Safari Books Online as their primary resource for research, problem solving, learning, and certification training.

Safari Books Online offers a range of plans and pricing for enterprise, government, education, and individuals.

Members have access to thousands of books, training videos, and prepublication manuscripts in one fully searchable database from publishers like O'Reilly Media, Prentice Hall Professional, Addison-Wesley Professional, Microsoft Press, Sams, Que, Peachpit Press, Focal Press, Cisco Press, John Wiley & Sons, Syngress, Morgan Kaufmann, IBM Redbooks, Packt, Adobe Press, FT Press, Apress, Manning, New Riders, McGraw-Hill, Jones & Bartlett, Course Technology, and hundreds more. For more information about Safari Books Online, please visit us online.

How to Contact Us

Please address comments and questions concerning this book to the publisher:

O'Reilly Media, Inc.
1005 Gravenstein Highway North
Sebastopol, CA 95472
800-998-9938 (in the United States or Canada)
707-829-0515 (international or local)
707-829-0104 (fax)

We have a web page for this book, where we list errata, examples, and any additional information. You can access this page at *http://bit.ly/building-isomorphic-javascript-apps*.

To comment or ask technical questions about this book, send email to *bookquestions@oreilly.com*.

For more information about our books, courses, conferences, and news, see our website at *http://www.oreilly.com*.

Find us on Facebook: *http://facebook.com/oreilly*

Follow us on Twitter: *http://twitter.com/oreillymedia*

Watch us on YouTube: *http://www.youtube.com/oreillymedia*

Acknowledgments

Jason Strimpel

First, I have to thank my wife Lasca for her patience and support. Every day I am grateful for your intellect, your humor, your compassion, and your love. I feel privileged and humbled that you chose to go through life with me. You make me an infinitely better person. Thanks for loving me.

Next, I would like to thank my coauthor and colleague Max. Without your passion, knowledge, ideas, and expertise my efforts would have fallen short. Your insights into software architecture and observations inspire me daily. Thank you.

I would also like to thank my editor Ally. Your ideas, questions, and edits make me appear to be a much better writer than I actually am in reality. Thank you.

Finally, I would like to thank all contributors to Part III who have graciously given their time and chosen to share their stories with the reader. Your chapters help showcase the depth of isomorphic JavaScript and the actual diversity of solutions. Your unique solutions illustrate the true ingenuity at the heart of every engineer. Thank you.

Maxime Najim

Foremost, I'd like to thank my family—my wife Nicole and our children Tatiana and Alexandra—for their support and encouragement throughout the writing and publishing of this book.

I'm also eternally grateful to Jason for asking me to coauthor this book with him. I felt privileged and honored to write and collaborate with you throughout this book. This was a once-in-a-lifetime opportunity, and it was your ingenuity, knowledge, and hard work that made this opportunity into a reality. I can't thank you enough. Likewise, a big thanks goes to our editor Allyson for her invaluable support and consultation throughout this process.

And finally, a big special thanks to the contributors to Part III who took time from their busy schedules to share their stories and experiences with us all. Thank you!

PART I

Introduction and Key Concepts

Ever since the term "Golden Age" originated with the early Greek and Roman poets, the phrase has been used to denote periods of time following certain technological advancements or innovations. In the Golden Ages of Radio and Television in the 20th century, writers and artists applied their skills to new mediums to create something fresh and compelling. Perhaps we are now in the Golden Age of JavaScript, although only time will tell. Beyond a doubt, JavaScript has paved the road toward a new age of desktop-like applications running in the browser.

In the past decade, we've seen the Web evolve as a platform for building rich and highly interactive applications. The web browser is no longer simply a document renderer, nor is the Web simply a bunch of documents linked together. *Websites* have evolved into *web apps*. This means more and more of the web app logic is running in the browser instead of on the server. Yet, in the past decade, we've equally seen user expectations evolve. The initial page load has become more critical than ever before. According to a Radware report (*http://bit.ly/radwarereport*), in 1999, the average user was willing to wait 8 seconds for a page to load. By 2010, 57% of online shoppers said that they would abandon a page after 3 seconds if nothing was shown. And here lies the problem of the Golden Age of JavaScript: the client-side JavaScript that makes the pages richer and more interactive also increases the page load times, creating a poor initial user experience. Page load times ultimately impact a company's "bottom line." Both Amazon.com and Walmart.com have reported that for every 100 milliseconds of improvement in their page load times, they were able to grow incremental revenue by up to 1% (*http://bit.ly/pageloadspeed*).

In Part I of this book we will discuss the concepts of isomorphic JavaScript and how isomorphic rendering can dramatically improve the user experience. We'll also discuss isomorphic JavaScript as a spectrum, looking at different categories of isomorphic code. Finally, we'll look beyond server-side rendering at how isomorphic JavaScript can help in creating complex, live-updating, and collaborative real-time applications.

CHAPTER 1

Why Isomorphic JavaScript?

Jason Strimpel and Maxime Najim

In 2010, Twitter released a new, rearchitected version of its site. This "#NewTwitter" pushed the UI rendering and logic to the JavaScript running in the user's browser. For its time, this architecture was groundbreaking. However, within two years, Twitter had released a re-rearchitected version of its site that moved the rendering back to the server. This allowed Twitter to drop the initial page load times to one-fifth of what they were previously (*http://bit.ly/twitterwebspeed*). Twitter's move back to server-side rendering caused quite a stir in the JavaScript community. What its developers and many others soon realized was that client-side rendering has a very noticeable impact on performance.

 The biggest weakness in building client-side web apps is the expensive initial download of large JavaScript files. TCP (Transmission Control Protocol), the prevailing transport of the Internet, has a congestion control mechanism called *slow start*, which means data is sent in an incrementally growing number of segments. Ilya Grigorik, in his book *High Performance Browser Networking* (O'Reilly), explains how it takes "four roundtrips... and hundreds of milliseconds of latency, to reach 64 KB of throughput between the client and server." Clearly, the first few KB of data sent to the user are essential to a great user experience and page responsiveness.

The rise of client-side JavaScript applications that consist of no markup other than a `<script>` tag and an empty `<body>` has created a broken Web of slow initial page loads, hashbang (#!) URL hacks (more on that later), and poor crawlability for search engines. Isomorphic JavaScript is about fixing this brokenness by consolidating the code base that runs on the client and the server. It's about providing the best from two different architectures and creating applications that are easier to maintain and provide better user experiences.

Defining Isomorphic JavaScript

Isomorphic JavaScript applications are simply applications that share the same Java-Script code between the browser client and the web application server. Such applications are isomorphic in the sense that they take on equal (*iso*) form or shape (*morphosis*) regardless of which environment they are running on, be it the client or the server. Isomorphic JavaScript is the next evolutionary step in the advancement of JavaScript. But advancements in software development often seem like a pendulum, accelerating toward an equilibrium position but always oscillating, swinging back and forth. If you've done software development for some time, you've likely seen design approaches come and go and come back again. It seems in some cases we're never able to find the right balance, a harmonious equilibrium between two opposite approaches.

This is most true with approaches to web application in the last two decades. We've seen the Web evolve from its humble roots of blue hyperlink text on a static page to rich user experiences that resemble full-blown native applications. This was made possible by a major swing in the web client–server model, moving rapidly from a fat-server, thin-client approach to a thin-server, fat-client approach. But this shift in approaches has created plenty of issues that we will discuss in greater detail later in this chapter. For now, suffice it to say there is a need for a harmonious equilibrium of a shared fat-client, fat-server approach. But in order to truly understand the significance of this equilibrium, we must take a step back and look at how web applications have evolved over the last few decades.

Evaluating Other Web Application Architecture Solutions

In order to understand why isomorphic JavaScript solutions came to be, we must first understand the climate from which the solutions arose. The first step is identifying the primary use case.

 Chapter 2 introduces two different types of isomorphic JavaScript application and examines their architectures. The primary type of isomorphic JavaScript that will be explored by this book is the ecommerce web application.

A Climate for Change

The creation of the World Wide Web is attributed to Tim Berners Lee (*https://www.w3.org/People/Berners-Lee/*), who, while working for a nuclear research company on a project known as "Enquire" (*http://en.wikipedia.org/wiki/ENQUIRE*) experimented with the concept of hyperlinks. In 1989, Tim applied the concept of hyperlinks and put a proposal together for a centralized database that contained links to other documents. Over the course of time, this database has morphed into something much larger and has had a huge impact on our daily lives (e.g., through social media) and business (ecommerce). We are all teenagers stuck in a virtual mall. The variety of content and shopping options empowers us to make informed decisions and purchases. Businesses realize the plethora of choices we have as consumers, and are greatly concerned with ensuring that we can find and view their content and products, with the ultimate goal of achieving conversions (buying stuff)—so much so that there are search engine optimization (SEO) experts whose only job is to make content and products appear higher in search results. However, that is not where the battle for conversions ends. Once consumers can find the products, the pages must load quickly and be responsive to user interactions, or else the businesses might lose the consumers to competitors. This is where we, engineers, enter the picture, and we have our own set of concerns in addition to the business's concerns.

Engineering Concerns

As engineers, we have a number of concerns, but for the most part these concerns fall into the main categories of maintainability and efficiency. That is not to say that we do not consider business concerns when weighing technical decisions. As a matter of fact, good engineers do exactly the opposite: they find the optimal engineering solution by contemplating the short- and long-term pros and cons of each possibility within the context of the business problem at hand.

Available Architectures

Taking into account the primary business use case, an ecommerce application, we are going to examine a couple of different architectures within the context of history. Before we take a look at the architectures, we should first identify some key acceptance criteria, so we can fairly evaluate the different architectures. In order of importance:

1. The application should be able to be indexed by search engines.

2. The application's first page load should be optimized—i.e., the *critical rendering path* should be part of the initial response.

3. The application should be responsive to user interactions (e.g., optimized page transitions).

The critical rendering path is the content that is related to the primary action a user wants to take on the page. In the case of an ecommerce application it would be a product description. In the case of a news site it would be an article's content.

These business criteria will also be weighed against the primary engineering concerns, maintainability and efficiency, throughout the evaluation process.

Classic web application

As mentioned in the previous section, the Web was designed and created to share information. Since the premise of the World Wide Web was the work done for the Enquire project, it is no surprise that when the Web first started, web pages were simply multipage text documents that linked to other text documents. In the early 1990s, most of the Web was rendered as complete HTML pages. The mechanisms that supported (and continue to support) it are HTML, URIs, and HTTP. HTML (Hypertext Markup Language) is the specification for the markup that is translated into the document object model by browsers when the markup is parsed. The URI (uniform resource identifier) is the name that identifies a resource; i.e., the name of the server that should respond to a request. HTTP (Hypertext Transfer Protocol) is the transport protocol that connects everything together. These three mechanisms power the Internet and shaped the architecture of the classic web application.

A classic web application is one in which all the markup—or, at a minimum, the critical rendering path markup—is rendered by the server using a server-side language such as PHP, Ruby, Java, and so on (Figure 1-1). Then JavaScript is initialized when the browser parses the document, enriching the user experience.

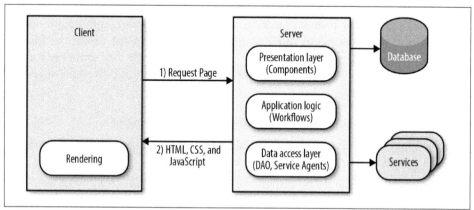

Figure 1-1. Classic web application flow

In a nutshell, that is the classic web application architecture. Let's see how it stacks up against our acceptance criteria and engineering concerns.

Firstly, it is easily indexed by search engines because all of the content is available when the crawlers traverse the application, so consumers can find the application's content. Secondly, the page load is optimized because the critical rendering path markup is rendered by the server, which improves the perceived rendering speed, so users are more likely not to bounce from the application. However, two out of three is as good as it gets for the classic web application.

 What do we mean by "perceived" rendering speed? In *High Performance Browser Networking*, Grigorik explains it this way as: "Time is measured objectively but perceived subjectively, and experiences can be engineered to improve perceived performance."

In the classic web application, navigation and transfer of data work as the Web was originally designed. The browser requests, receives, and parses a full document response when a user navigates to a new page or submits form data, even if only some of the page information has changed. This is extremely effective at meeting the first two criteria, but the setup and teardown of this full-page lifecycle are extremely costly, so it is a suboptimal solution in terms of responsiveness. Since we are privileged enough to live in the time of Ajax, we already know that there is a more efficient method than a full page reload—but it comes at a cost, which we will explore in the next section. However, before we transition to the next section we should take a look at Ajax within the context of the classic web application architecture.

The Ajax era. The `XMLHttpRequest` (*http://bit.ly/xmlhttpreq*) object is the spark that ignited the web platform fire. However, its integration into classic web applications has been less impressive. This was not due to the design or technology itself, but rather to the inexperience of those who integrated the technology into classic web applications. In most cases they were designers who began to specialize in the view layer. I myself was an administrative assistant turned designer and developer. I was abysmal at both. Needless to say, I wreaked havoc on my share of applications over the years (but I see this as my contribution to the evolution of a platform!). Unfortunately, all the applications I touched and all the other applications that those of us without the proper training and guidance touched suffered during this evolutionary period. The applications suffered because processes were duplicated and concerns were muddled. A good example that highlights these issues is a related products carousel (Figure 1-2).

Figure 1-2. Example of a product carousel

A (related) products carousel paginates through products. Sometimes all the products are preloaded, and in other cases there are too many to preload. In those cases a network request is made to paginate to the next set of products. Refreshing the entire page is extremely inefficient, so the typical solution is to use Ajax to fetch the product page sets when paginating. The next optimization would be to only get the data required to render the page set, which would require duplicating templates, models, assets, and rendering on the client (Figure 1-3). This also necessitates more unit tests. This is a very simple example, but if you take the concept and extrapolate it over a large application, it makes the application difficult to follow and maintain—one cannot easily derive how an application ended up in a given state. Additionally, the duplication is a waste of resources and it opens up an application to the possibility of bugs being introduced across two UI code bases when a feature is added or modified.

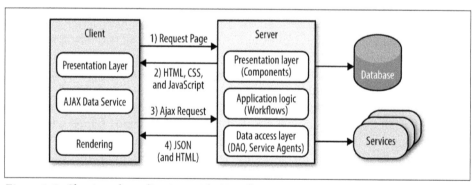

Figure 1-3. Classic web application with Ajax flow

This division and replication of the UI/View layer, enabled by Ajax and coupled with the best of intentions, is what turned seemingly well-constructed applications into brittle, regression-prone piles of rubble and frustrated numerous engineers. Fortunately, frustrated engineers are usually the most innovative. It was this frustration-fueled innovation, combined with solid engineering skills, that led us to the next application architecture.

Single-page web application

Everything moves in cycles. When the Web began it was a thin client, and likely the inspiration for the Sun Microsystems NetWork Terminal (*http://en.wikipedia.org/wiki/Sun_Ray*) (NeWT). But by 2011 web applications had started to eschew the thin client model, and transition to a fat client model like their operating system counterparts had done long ago. The monolith had surfaced. It was the dawn of the single-page application (SPA) architecture.

The SPA eliminates the issues that plague classic web applications by shifting the responsibility of rendering entirely to the client. This model separates application logic from data retrieval, consolidates UI code to a single language and runtime, and significantly reduces the impact on the servers (Figure 1-4).

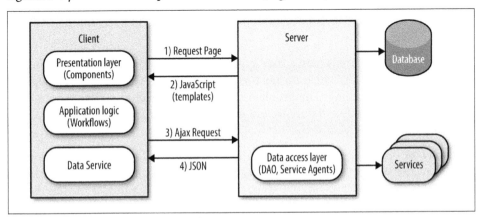

Figure 1-4. Single-page application flow

It accomplishes this reduction because the server sends a payload of assets, JavaScript, and templates to the client. From there, the client takes over only fetching the data it needs to render pages/views. This behavior significantly improves the rendering of pages because it does not require the overhead of fetching and parsing an entire document when a user requests a new page or submits data. In addition to the performance gains, this model also solves the engineering concerns that Ajax introduced to the classic web application.

Going back to the product carousel example, the first page of the (related) products carousel was rendered by the application server. Upon pagination, subsequent requests were then rendered by the client. The blurring of the lines of responsibility and duplication of efforts evidenced here are the primary problems of the classic web application in the modern web platform. These issues do not exist in an SPA.

In an SPA there is a clear line of separation between the responsibilities of the server and client. The API server responds to data requests, the application server supplies the static resources, and the client runs the show. In the case of the products carousel, an empty document that contains a payload of JavaScript and template resources would be sent by the application server to the browser. The client application would then initialize in the browser and request the data required to render the view that contains the products carousel. After receiving the data, the client application would render the first set of items for the carousel. Upon pagination, the data fetching and rendering lifecycle would repeat, following the same code path. This is an outstanding engineering solution. Unfortunately, it is not always the best user experience.

In an SPA the initial page load can appear extremely sluggish to the end users, because they have to wait for the data to be fetched before the page can be rendered. So instead of seeing content immediately when the pages loads, they get an animated loading indicator, at best. A common approach to mitigate this delayed rendering is to serve the data for the initial page. However, this requires application server logic, so it begins to blur the lines of responsibility once again and adds another layer of code to maintain.

The next issue SPAs face is both a user experience and a business issue. They are not SEO-friendly by default, which means that users will not be able to find an application's content by searching. The problem stems from the fact that SPAs leverage the hash fragment for routing. Before we examine why this impacts SEO, let's take a look at the mechanics of SPA routing.

SPAs rely on the fragment to map faux URI paths to a route handler that renders a view in response. For example, in a classic web application an "about us" page URI might look like *http://domain.com/about*, but in an SPA it would look like *http://domain.com/#about*. The SPA uses a hash mark and a fragment identifier at the end of the URL. The reason the SPA router uses the fragment is because the browser does not make a network request when the fragment changes, unlike when there are changes to the URI. This is important because the whole premise of the SPA is that it only requests the data required to render a view/page, as opposed to fetching and parsing a new document for each page.

SPA fragments are not SEO-compatible because hash fragments are never sent to the server as part of the HTTP request (per the specification). As far as a web crawler is concerned, *http://domain.com/#about* and *http://domain.com/#faqs* are the same page. Fortunately, Google has implemented a work around to provide SEO support for fragments: the hashbang (*#!*).

 Most SPA libraries now support the History API (*http://bit.ly/apih ist*), and recently Google crawlers have gotten better at indexing JavaScript applications—previously, JavaScript was not even executed by web crawlers.

The basic premise is to replace the # in an SPA fragment's route with a #!, so *http://domain.com/#about* would become *http://domain.com/#!about*. This allows the Google crawler to identify content to be indexed from simple anchors.

 An anchor tag is used to create links to the content within the body of a document.

The crawler then transforms the links into fully qualified URI versions, so *http://domain.com/#!about* becomes *http://domain.com/?query&_escaped_fragment=about*. At that point it is the responsibility of the server that hosts the SPA to serve a snapshot of the HTML that represents *http://domain.com/#!about* to the crawler in response to the URI *http://domain.com/?query&_escaped_fragment=about*. Figure 1-5 illustrates this process.

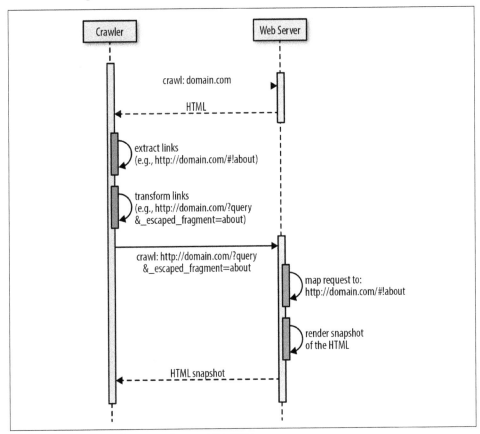

Figure 1-5. Crawler flow to index an SPA URI

At this point, the value proposition of the SPA begins to decline even more. From an engineering perspective, one is left with two options:

1. Spin up the server with a headless browser, such as PhantomJS (*http://phan tomjs.org/*), to run the SPA on the server to handle crawler requests.

2. Outsource the problem to a third-party provider, such as BromBone (*http://www.brombone.com/*).

Both potential SEO fixes come at a cost, and this is in addition to the suboptimal first page rendering mentioned earlier. Fortunately, engineers love to solve problems. So just as the SPA was an improvement over the classic web application, so was born the next architecture, isomorphic JavaScript.

Isomorphic JavaScript applications

Isomorphic JavaScript applications are the perfect union of the classic web application and single-page application architectures. They offer:

- SEO support using fully qualified URIs by default—no more #! workaround required—via the History API, and graceful fallbacks to server rendering for clients that don't support the History API when navigating.

- Distributed rendering of the SPA model for subsequent page requests for clients that support the History API. This approach also lessens server loads.

- A single code base for the UI with a common rendering lifecycle. No duplication of efforts or blurring of the lines. This reduces the UI development costs, lowers bug counts, and allows you to ship features faster.

- Optimized page load by rendering the first page on the server. No more waiting for network calls and displaying loading indicators before the first page renders.

- A single JavaScript stack, which means that the UI application code (*http://bit.ly/nodejsweb*) can be maintained by frontend engineers versus frontend and backend engineers. Clear separation of concerns and responsibilities means that experts contribute code only to their respective areas.

The isomorphic JavaScript architecture meets all three of the key acceptance criteria outlined at the beginning of this section. Isomorphic JavaScript applications are easily indexed by all search engines, have an optimized page load, and have optimized page transitions (in modern browsers that support the History API; this gracefully degrades in legacy browsers with no impact on application architecture).

Caveat: When Not to Go Isomorphic

Companies like Yahoo!, Facebook, Netflix, and Airbnb, to name a few, have embraced isomorphic JavaScript. However, isomorphic JavaScript architecture might suit some applications more than others. As we'll explore in this book, isomorphic JavaScript apps require additional architectural considerations and implementation complexity. For single-page applications that are not performance-critical and do not have SEO requirements (like applications behind a login), isomorphic JavaScript might seem like more trouble than it's worth.

Likewise, many companies and organizations might not be in a situation in which they are prepared to operate and maintain a JavaScript execution engine on the server side. For example, Java-, Ruby-, Python-, or PHP-heavy shops might lack the know-how for monitoring and troubleshooting JavaScript application servers (e.g., Node.js) in production. In such cases, isomorphic JavaScript might present an additional operational cost that is not easily taken on.

 Node.js provides a remarkable server-side JavaScript runtime. For servers using Java, Ruby, Python, or PHP, there are two main alternative options: 1) run a Node.js process alongside the normal server as a local or remote "render service," or 2) use an embedded JavaScript runtime (e.g., Nashorn, which comes packaged with Java 8). However, there are clear downsides to these approaches. Running Node.js as a render service adds an additional overhead cost of serializing data over a communication socket. Likewise, using an embedded JavaScript runtime in languages that are traditionally not optimized for JavaScript execution can offer additional performance challenges (although this may improve over time).

If your project or company does not require what isomorphic JavaScript architecture offers (as outlined in this chapter), then by all means, use the right tool for the job. However, when server-side rendering is no longer optional and initial page load performance and search engine optimization do become concerns for you, don't worry; this book will be right here, waiting for you.

Summary

In this chapter we defined isomorphic JavaScript applications—applications that share the same JavaScript code for both the browser client and the web application server—and identified the primary type of isomorphic JavaScript app that we'll be covering in this book: the ecommerce web application. We then took a stroll back through history and saw how other architectures evolved, weighing the architectures against the key acceptance criteria of SEO support, optimized first page load, and optimized page transitions. We saw that the architectures that preceded isomorphic JavaScript did not meet all of these acceptance criteria. We ended the chapter with the merging of two architectures, the classic web application and the single-page application, which resulted in the isomorphic JavaScript architecture.

Isomorphic JavaScript as a Spectrum

Maxime Najim

Isomorphic JavaScript is a spectrum (Figure 2-1). On one side of the spectrum, the client and server share minimal bits of view rendering (like Handlebars.js templates); some name, date, or URL formatting code; or some parts of the application logic. At this end of the spectrum we mostly find a shared client and server view layer with shared templates and helper functions (Figure 2-2). These applications require fewer abstractions, since many useful libraries found in popular JavaScript libraries like Underscore.js (*http://underscorejs.org*) or Lodash.js (*https://lodash.com*) can be shared between the client and the server.

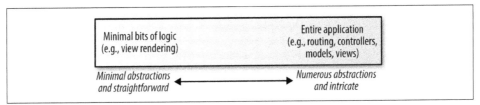

Figure 2-1. Isomorphic JavaScript as a spectrum

On the other side of this spectrum, the client and server share the entire application (Figure 2-3). This includes sharing the entire view layer, application flows, user access constraints, form validations, routing logic, models, and states. These applications require more abstractions since the client code is executing in the context of the DOM (document object model) and window, whereas the server works in the context of a request/response object.

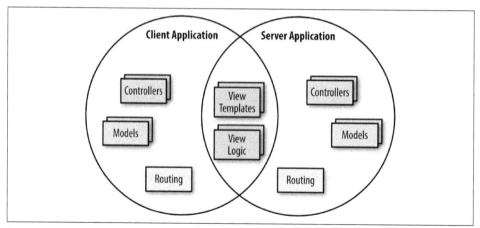

Figure 2-2. Sharing the view layer

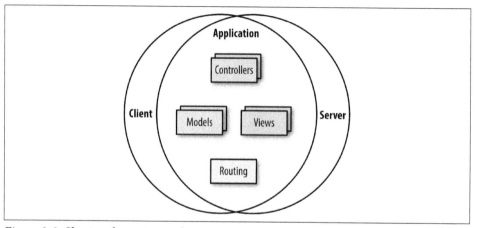

Figure 2-3. Sharing the entire application

 In Part II of this book we will dive into the mechanics of sharing code between the client and server. However, as a form of introduction, this chapter will briefly explore the two ends of the spectrum by looking at various functional application pieces that can be shared between the client and server (we will also point out some of the abstractions required to allow these functional pieces to work isomorphically).

Sharing Views

Single-page applications (SPAs) provide users with a more fluid experience by reducing the total number of full page reloads that they must experience as they navigate from one page to another. Instead, SPAs partially render parts of a page as a result of user interaction. SPAs utilize client-side template engines for taking a template (with simple placeholders) and executing it against a model object to output HTML that can be attached to the DOM. Client-side templates help separate the view markup from the view logic to create more maintainable code. Sharing views isomorphically means sharing both the template and the view logic associated with those templates.

Sharing Templates

In order to achieve faster (perceived) performance and proper search engine indexing, we want to be able to render any view on the server as well as the client. On the client, template rendering is as simple as evaluating a template and attaching the output to a DOM element. On the server, the same template is rendered as a string and returned in the response. The tricky part of isomorphic view rendering is that the client has to pick up wherever the server left off. This is often called the *client/server transition*; that is, the client should properly transition and not "destroy" the DOM generated by the server after the application is loaded in the browser. The server needs to "dehydrate" the state by sending it to the client, and the client will "rehydrate" (or reanimate) the view and initialize it to the same state it was in on the server.

Example 2-1 illustrates a typical response from the server, which has the rendered markup in the body of the page and the serialized state within a `<script>` tag. The server puts the serialized state in the rendered view, and the client will deserialize the state and attach it to the prerendered markup.

Example 2-1. Including server-side rendered markup and state

```
<html>
  <body>
    <div>[[server_side_rendered_markup]]</div>
    <script>window.__state__=[[serialized_state]<]/script>
    ...
  </body>
</html>
```

Sharing View Logic

Template helpers are objects, like numbers, strings, or hash objects, and are typically easy to share. For sharing formatting like dates, many formatting libraries work both on the server and on the client. Moment.js, for example, can parse, validate, manipulate, and display dates in JavaScript both on the server and on the client. URL formatting, on the other hand, requires prepending the host and port to the path, whereas on the client we can simply use the relative URL.

Sharing Routes

Most modern SPA frameworks support the concept of a router, which tracks the user's state as she navigates from one view or page to another. In an SPA, routing is the main mechanism needed for handling navigation events, changing the state and view of the page, and updating the browser's navigation history. In an isomorphic application, we also need a set of routing configurations (i.e., a map of URI patterns to route handlers) that are easily shared between the server and the client. The challenge of sharing routes is found in the route handlers themselves, since they often need access to environment APIs that require accessing URL information, HTTP headers, and cookies. On the server this information is accessed via the request object's APIs, whereas on the client the browser's APIs are used instead.

Sharing Models

Models are often referred to as business/domain objects or entities. Models establish an abstraction for data by removing state storage and retrieval from the DOM. In the simplest approach, an isomorphic application initializes the client in the exact same state it was in on the server before being sent back the initial page response. At the extreme end of the isomorphic JavaScript spectrum, sharing the state and specification of the models includes two-way synchronization of state between the server and the client (please see Chapter 4 for a further exploration of this approach).

Summary

Applications can differ in their position on the isomorphic JavaScript spectrum. The amount of code shared between the server and the client can vary, starting from sharing templates, to sharing the application's entire view layer, all the way up to sharing the majority of the application's logic. As applications progress along the isomorphic spectrum, more abstractions need to be created. In the next chapter we will discuss the different categories of isomorphic JavaScript and dive deeper into these abstractions.

CHAPTER 3

Different Categories of Isomorphic JavaScript

Maxime Najim

Charlie Robbins is commonly credited for coining the term "isomorphic JavaScript" in a 2011 blog post entitled "Scaling Isomorphic Javascript Code" (*http://bit.ly/scalingisojs*). The term was later popularized by Spike Brehm in a 2013 blog post entitled "Isomorphic JavaScript: The Future of Web Apps" (*http://nerds.airbnb.com/isomorphic-javascript-future-web-apps/*) along with subsequent articles and conference talks. However, there has been some contention over the word "isomorphic" in the JavaScript community (*http://bit.ly/renamingisojs*). Michael Jackson, a React.js trainer and coauthor of the react-router project, has suggested the term "universal" JavaScript (*http://bit.ly/universaljs*). Jackson argues that the term "universal" highlights JavaScript code that can run "not only on servers and browsers, but on native devices and embedded architectures as well."

"Isomorphism," on the other hand, is a mathematical term, which captures the notion of two mathematical objects that have corresponding or similar forms when we simply ignore their individual distinctions. When applying this mathematical concept to graph theory, it becomes easy to visualize. Take for example the two graphs in Figure 3-1.

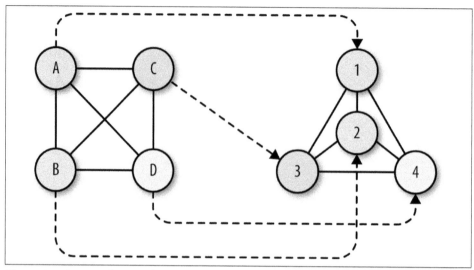

Figure 3-1. Isomorphic graphs

These graphs are isomorphic, even though they look very different. The two graphs have the same number of nodes, with each node having the same number of edges. But what makes them isomorphic is that there exists a mapping for each node from the first graph to a corresponding node in the second graph while maintaining certain properties. For example, the node A can be mapped to node 1 while maintaining its adjacency in the second graph. In fact, all nodes in the first graph have an exact one-to-one correspondence to nodes in the second graph while maintaining adjacency.

This is what is nice about the "isomorphic" analogy. In order for JavaScript code to run in both the client and server environments, these environments have to be isomorphic; that is, there should exist a mapping of the client environment's functionality to the server environment, and vice versa. Just as the two isomorphic graphs shown in Figure 3-1 have a mapping, so do isomorphic JavaScript environments.

JavaScript code that does not depend on environment-specific features—for example, code that avoids using the `window` or `request` objects—can easily run on both sides of the wire. But for JavaScript code that accesses environment-specific properties—e.g., `req.path` or `window.location.pathname`—a mapping (sometimes referred to as a "shim") needs to be provided to abstract or "fill in" a given environment-specific property. This leads us to two general categories of isomorphic JavaScript: 1) environment agnostic and 2) shimmed for each environment.

Environment Agnostic

Environment-agnostic node modules use only pure JavaScript functionality, and no environment-specific APIs or properties like window (for the client) and process (for the server). Examples are Lodash.js, Async.js, Moment.js, Numeral.js, Math.js, and Handlebars.js, to name a few. Many modules fall into this category, and they simply work out of the box in an isomorphic application.

The only thing we need to address with these kinds of Node modules is that they use Node's require(*module_id*) module loader. Browsers don't support the node require(..) method. To deal with this, we need to use a build tool that will compile the Node modules for the browser. There are two main build tools that do just that: namely, Browserify and Webpack.

In Example 3-1, we use Moment.js to define a date formatter that will run on both the server and the client.

Example 3-1. Defining an isomorphic date formatter

```
'use strict';

var moment = require('moment');  //Node-specific require statement

var formatDate = function(date) {
    return moment(date).format('MMMM Do YYYY, h:mm:ss a');
};

module.exports = formatDate
```

We also have a simple *main.js* that will call the `formatDate(..)` function to format the current time:

```
var formatDate = require('./dateFormatter.js');
console.log(formatDate(Date.now()));
```

When we run *main.js* on the server (using Node.js), we get the output like the following:

```
$ node main.js
July 25th 2015, 11:27:27 pm
```

Browserify (*http://browserify.org*) is a tool for compiling CommonJS modules by bundling up all the required Node modules for the browser. Using Browserify, we can output a bundled JavaScript file that is browser-friendly:

```
$ browserify main.js > bundle.js
```

When we open the *bundle.js* file in a browser, we can see the same date message in the browser's console (Figure 3-2).

```
<script src="bundle.js"></script>
```

Figure 3-2. Browser console output when running bundle.js

Pause for a second and think about what just happened. This is a simple example, but you can see the astonishing ramifications. With a simple build tool, we can easily share logic between the server and the client with very little effort. This opens many possibilities that we'll dive deeper into in Part II of this book.

Shimmed for Each Environment

There are many differences between client- and server-side JavaScript. On the client there are global objects like `window` and different APIs like localStorage, the History API, and WebGL. On the server we are working in the context of a request/response lifecycle and the server has its own global objects.

Running the following code in the browser returns the current URL location of the browser. Changing the value of this property will redirect the page:

```
console.log(window.location.href);
window.location.href = 'http://www.oreilly.com'
```

Running that same code on the server returns an error:

```
> console.log(window.location.href);
ReferenceError: window is not defined
```

This makes sense since `window` is not a global object on the server. In order to do the same redirect on the server we must write a header to the response object with a status code to indicate a URL redirection (e.g., 302) and the `location` that the client will navigate to:

```
var http = require('http');
http.createServer(function (req, res) {
  console.log(req.path);
  res.writeHead(302, {'Location': 'http://www.oreilly.com'});
  res.end();
}).listen(1337, '127.0.0.1');
```

As we can see, the server code looks much different from the client code. So, then, how do we run the same code on both sides of the wire?

We have two options. The first option is to extract the redirect logic into a separate module that is aware of which environment it is running in. The rest of the application code simply calls this module, being completely agnostic to the environment-specific implementation:

```
var redirect = require('shared-redirect');

// Do some interesting application logic that decides if a redirect is required

if(isRedirectRequired){
  redirect('http://www.oreilly.com');
}

// Continue with interesting application logic
```

With this approach the application logic becomes environment agnostic and can run on both the client and the server. The `redirect(..)` function implementation needs to account for the environment-specific implementations, but this is self-contained and does not bleed into the rest of the application logic. Here is a possible implementation of the `redirect(..)` function:

```
if (window) {
  window.location.href = 'http://www.oreilly.com'
} else {
  this._res.writeHead(302, {'Location': 'http://www.oreilly.com'});
}
```

Notice that this function must be aware of the `window` implementation and must use it accordingly.

The alternative approach is to simply use the server's response interface on the client, but shimmed to use the `window` property instead. This way, the application code always calls `res.writeHead(..)`, but in the browser this will be shimmed to call the `window.location.href` property. We will look into this approach in more detail in Part II of this book.

Summary

In this chapter, we looked at two different categories of isomorphic JavaScript code. We saw how easy it is to simply port environment-agnostic Node modules to the browser using a tool like Browserify. We also saw how environment-specific implementations can be shimmed for each environment to allow code to be reused on the client and the server. It's now time to take it to the next level. In the next chapter we'll go beyond server-side rendering and look at how isomorphic JavaScript can be used for different solutions. We'll explore innovative, forward-looking application architectures that use isomorphic JavaScript to accomplish novel things.

CHAPTER 4

Going Beyond Server-Side Rendering

Maxime Najim

Applications come in different shapes and sizes. In the introductory chapters we focused mainly on single-page applications that can also be rendered on the server. The server renders the initial page to improve perceived page load time and for search engine optimization (SEO). That discussion was focused around the classic application architecture, in which the client initiates a REST call and is routed to one of the stateless backend servers, which in turn queries the database and returns the data to the client (Figure 4-1).

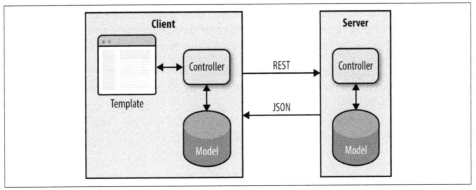

Figure 4-1. Classic web application architecture

This approach is great for classic ecommerce web applications. But there is another class of applications, often referred to as "real-time" applications. In fact, we can say that there are two classes of isomorphic JavaScript applications: single-page apps that can be server-rendered and apps that use isomorphic JavaScript for real-time, offline, and data-syncing capabilities.

Matt Debergalis has described real-time applications as a natural evolutionary step in the rich history of application architectures. He believes that changes in application architecture are driven by new eras of cheap CPUs, the Internet, and the emergence of mobile. Each of these changes resulted in the development of new application architectures. However, even though we are seeing more complex, live-updating, and collaborative real-time applications, the majority of applications remain single-page apps that can benefit from server-side rendering. Nonetheless, we feel this subject is important to the future of application architecture and very relevant to our discussion of isomorphic JavaScript applications.

Real-Time Web Applications

Real-time applications have a rich interactive interface and a collaborative element that allows users to share data with other users. Think of a chat application like Slack; a shared document application like Google Docs; or a ride-share application like Uber, which shows all the available drivers and their locations in real time to all the users. For these kinds of applications we end up designing and implementing ways to push data from the server to the client to show other users' changes as they happen. We also need a way to reactively update the screen on each client once that data comes from the server. Most of these real-time applications have similar functional pieces. These applications must have some mechanism for watching a database for changes, some kind of protocol that runs on top of a push technology like WebSockets to push data to the client (or emulate server data pushes using long polling—i.e., where the server holds the request open until new data is available and has been sent), and some kind of cache on the client to avoid the round-trips to the server when redrawing the screen.

In Figure 4-2 we can see how data flows from the user's interaction with the view. We can also see how changes from other clients propagate to all users and how the view rerenders when data changes are sent from the server. There are three interesting isomorphic concepts that come up in this kind of architecture: isomorphic APIs, bidirectional data synchronization, and client simulation on the server.

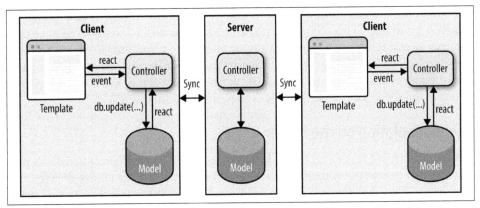

Figure 4-2. Real-time web application architecture

Isomorphic APIs

In an isomorphic real-time application, the client interacts with its local data cache similarly to how the server interacts with the backing database. The server code is executing a statement against a database. That same statement is executed on the client to fetch data out of an in-memory cache using the same database API. This symmetry between client and server APIs is often referred to as *isomorphic APIs*. Isomorphic APIs relieve the developer from having to juggle different strategies for accessing data. But more importantly, isomorphic APIs make it possible to run an application's core business logic (especially across the model layer) and rendering logic on both the client and the server. Having an isomorphic API for accessing data allows us to share server code and the client application code for validating the updates to the data, accessing and storing the data, and transforming data. By using a consistent API, we remove the friction of having to write different variations of doing the same thing, having to test it in different ways, and having to update code twice when we need to change the data model. Isomorphic APIs are about being intelligent by following the DRY (Don't Repeat Yourself) principle.

Bidirectional Data Synchronization

Another important aspect of real-time applications is the synchronization between the server's database and the client's local cache. Updates to the server from a client should be updated in the client's local cache, and vice versa. Meteor.js is a good example of a real-time isomorphic framework that lets developers write JavaScript that runs on both the server and the client. Meteor has a "Database Everywhere" principle. Both the client and the server in Meteor use the same isomorphic APIs to access the database. Meteor also uses database abstractions, like minimongo, on the client and an observable collection over a DDP (dynamic data protocol) to keep the data in sync between the server and the client. It is the client database (not the server database) that drives the UI. The client database does lazy data synchronizing to keep the server database up to date. This allows the client to be offline and to still process user data changes locally. A write on the client can optionally be a speculative write to the client's local cache before hearing a confirmation back from the server. Meteor has a built-in latency compensation mechanism for refreshing the speculative cache if any writes to the server's database fail or are overwritten by another client.

Client Simulation on the Server

Taking isomorphic JavaScript to the extreme, real-time isomorphic applications may run separate processes on the server for each client session. This allows the server to look at the data that the application loads and proactively send data to the client, essentially simulating the UI on the server. This technique has been famously used by the Asana (*https://asana.com/*) application. Asana is a collaborative project management tool built on an in-house, closed-source framework called Luna. Luna is tailored for writing real-time web applications and is similar to Meteor.js in providing a common isomorphic API for accessing data on the client and the server. However, what makes Luna unique is that it runs a complete copy of the application on the server. Luna simulates the client on the server by executing the same JavaScript code on the server that is running in the client. As a user clicks around in the Asana UI, the JavaScript events in the client are synchronized with the server. The server maintains an exact copy of the user state by executing all the views and events, but simply throws away the HTML.

A recent post on Asana's engineering blog (*http://bit.ly/lunaframework*) indicates that Asana is moving away from this kind of client/server simulation, though. Performance is an issue, especially when the server has to simulate the UI in multiple states so that it can anticipate and preload data on the client for immediate availability. The post also cites versioning as an issue for mobile clients that may run older versions of the code, which makes simulation tricky since the client and the server are not running exactly the same code.

Summary

Isomorphic JavaScript is an attempt to share an application on both sides of the wire. By looking at real-time isomorphic frameworks, we have seen different solutions to sharing application logic. These frameworks take a more novel approach than simply taking a single-page application and rendering it on the server. There has been a lot of discussion around these concepts, and we hope this has provided a good introduction to the many facets of isomorphic JavaScript. In the next part of the book, we will build on these key concepts and create our first isomorphic application.

PART II

Building Our First App

Knowing what, when, and where to abstract is key to good software design. If you abstract too much and too soon, then you add layers of complexity that add little value, if any. If you do not abstract enough and in the right places, then you end up with a solution that is brittle and won't scale. When you have the perfect balance, it is truly beautiful. This is the art of software design, and engineers appreciate it like an art critic appreciates a good Picasso or Rembrandt.

In this part of the book we will attempt to create something of beauty. Many others have blazed the path ahead of us. Some have gotten it right and some have gotten it wrong. I have had experiences in both categories, with many more failures than successes, but with each failure I have learned a lesson or two. Armed with the knowledge gained from these lessons I will lead us through the precarious process of designing and implementing a lightweight isomorphic JavaScript application framework.

This will not be an easy process—most people get the form, structure, and abstractions wrong—but I am up for the challenge if you are. In the end, we may not have achieved perfection, but we will have learned lessons that we can apply to our future isomorphic JavaScript endeavors and we will have a nice base from which we can expand. After all, this is just a step in the evolution of software and us. Are you with me? Well then, let's push forward and blaze our own path from the ground up.

CHAPTER 5

Getting Started

Jason Strimpel

Now that we have a solid understanding of isomorphic JavaScript, it's time to go from theory to practice! In this chapter we lay the foundation that we'll progressively build upon until we have a fully functioning isomorphic application. This foundation will be comprised of the following main technologies:

- Node.js (*https://nodejs.org/*) will be the server runtime for our application. It is a platform built on Chrome's JavaScript runtime for easily building fast, scalable network applications. Node.js uses an event-driven, nonblocking I/O model that makes it lightweight and efficient, perfect for data-intensive real-time applications that run across distributed devices.

- Hapi.js (*http://hapijs.com/*) will be used to power the HTTP application server portion of our application. It is a rich framework for building applications and services. Hapi.js enables developers to focus on writing reusable application logic rather than spending time building infrastructure.

- Gulp.js (*http://gulpjs.com/*) will be used to compile our JavaScript (ES6 to ES5), create bundles for the browser, and manage our development workflow. It is a streaming build system based on Node streams: file manipulation is all done in memory, and it doesn't write any files until you tell it to do so.

- Babel.js (*https://babeljs.io/*) will allow us to begin leveraging ES6 syntax and features now by compiling our code to an ES5-compatible distributable. It is the compiler for writing next-generation JavaScript.

ES6 Versus ES2015

ES6 is also known as ES2015. Changing the name from ES6 to ES2015 happened late in the specification drafting and approval process, so the version is commonly known as ES6. In this book it will be referred to as ES6. To learn more about JavaScript version naming conventions, see "ECMAScript 6 support in Mozilla" (*http://bit.ly/ecmas criptsix*).

Installing the Project

If you are already comfortable with using Node, npm, and Gulp then feel free to skip this chapter and install the project that is the end result by running npm install thaumoctopus-mimicus@"0.1.x".

Getting Node Up and Running

Installing Node is very easy. Node will run on Linux, Mac OS, Windows, and Unix. You can install it from source via the terminal, using a package manager (e.g., yum, homebrew, apt-get, etc.), or by using one of the installers for Mac OS or Windows.

Installing from Source

This section outlines how to install Node from source. I highly recommend using one of the installers or a package manager, but if you are one of those rare birds who enjoy installing software from source, then this is the section for you. Otherwise, jump ahead to "Interacting with the Node REPL" on page 33.

The first step is to download the source from Nodejs.org:

```
$ wget http://nodejs.org/dist/v0.12.15/node-v0.12.15.tar.gz
```

Node Version

node-v0.12.15.tar.gz was the latest stable version at the time of writing. Check *https://nodejs.org/download/release/* for a more recent version and replace v0.12.15 in the URL of the wget example with the latest stable version.

Next, you'll need to extract the source in the downloaded file:

```
$ tar zxvf node-v0.12.15.tar.gz
```

This command unzips and extracts the Node source. For more information on the tar command options, execute man tar in your terminal.

Now that you have the source code on your computer, you need to run the configuration script in the source code directory. This script finds the required Node dependencies on your system and informs you if any are missing on your computer:

```
$ cd node-v0.12.15
$ ./configure
```

Once all dependencies have been found, the source code can then be compiled to a binary. This is done using the make command:

```
$ make
```

The last step is to run the make install command. This installs Node globally and requires sudo privileges:

```
$ sudo make install
```

If everything went smoothly, you should see output like the following when you check the Node.js version:

```
$ node -v
v0.12.15
```

Interacting with the Node REPL

Node is a runtime environment with a REPL (read–eval–print loop), which is a JavaScript shell that allows one to write JavaScript code and have it evaluated upon pressing Enter. It is like having the console from the Chrome developer tools in your terminal. You can try it out by entering a few basic commands:

```
$ node
> (new Date()).getTime();
1436887590047
>
(^C again to quit)
>
$
```

This is useful for testing out code snippets and debugging.

Managing Projects with npm

npm (*https://www.npmjs.com/*) is the package manager for Node. It allows developers to easily reuse their code across projects and share their code with other developers. npm comes packaged with Node, so when you installed Node you also installed npm:

```
$ npm -v
2.7.0
```

There are numerous tutorials and extensive documentation (*https://docs.npmjs.com/*) on the Web for npm, which is beyond the scope of this book. In the examples in the book we will primarily be working with *package.json* files, which contain metadata for the project, and the init and install commands. We'll use our application project as working example for learning how to leverage npm.

Setting Up the Application Project

Aside from source control, having a way to package, share, and deploy your code is one of the most important aspects of managing a software project. In this section, we will be using npm to set up our project.

Initializing the Project

The npm CLI (command-line interface) is terminal program that allows you to quickly execute commands that help you manage your project/package. One of these commands is init.

If you are already familiar with npm init or if you prefer to just take a look at the source code, then feel free to skip ahead to "Installing the Application Server" on page 36.

init is an interactive command that will ask you a series of questions and create a *package.json* file for your project. This file contains the metadata for your project (package name, version, dependencies, etc.). This metadata is used to publish your package to the npm repository and to install your package from the repository. Let's take a walk through the command:

```
$ npm init
This utility will walk you through creating a package.json file.
It only covers the most common items, and tries to guess sane defaults.

See `npm help json` for definitive documentation on these fields
and exactly what they do.

Use `npm install <pkg> --save` afterwards to install a package and
save it as a dependency in the package.json file.

Press ^C at any time to quit.
```

Project Directory

The computer name, directory path, and username (fantastic-planet:thaumoctopus-mimicus jstrimpel $) in the terminal code examples have been omitted for brevity. All terminal commands from this point forward are executed from the project directory.

The first prompt you'll see is for the package name. This will default to the current directory name, which in our case is *thaumoctopus-mimicus*.

```
name: (thaumoctopus-mimicus)
```

Project Name

"thaumoctopus-mimicus" is the name of the project that we will be building throughout Part II. Each chapter will be pinned to a minor version. For example, this chapter will be 0.1.x.

Press enter to continue. The next prompt is for the version:

```
version: (0.0.0)
```

`0.0.0` will do fine for now since we are just getting started and there will not be anything of significance to publish for some time. The next prompt is for a description of your project:

```
description:
```

Enter "Isomorphic JavaScript application example". Next, you'll be asked for for the entry point of your project:

```
entry point: (index.js)
```

The entry point is the file that is loaded when a user includes your package in his source code. `index.js` will suffice for now. The next prompt is the for the `test` command. Leave it blank (we will not be covering testing because it is outside the scope of this book):

```
test command:
```

Next, you'll be prompted for the project's GitHub repository. The default provided here is *https://github.com/isomorphic-javascript-book/thaumoctopus-mimicus.git*, which is this project's repository. Yours will likely be blank.

```
git repository:
    (https://github.com/isomorphic-javascript-book/thaumoctopus-mimicus.git)
```

The next prompt is for keywords for the project:

```
keywords:
```

Enter "isomorphic javascript". Then you'll be asked for the author's name:

```
author:
```

Enter your name here. The final prompt is for the license. The default value will be `(ISC) MIT` or `(ISC)`, depending on the NPM version, which is what we want:

```
license: (ISC) MIT
```

If you navigate to the project directory you will now see a *package.json* file with the contents shown in Example 5-1.

Example 5-1. package.json created by npm init

```
{
  "name": "thaumoctopus-mimicus",
  "version": "0.0.0",
  "description": "Isomorphic JavaScript application example",
  "main": "index.js",
  "scripts": {
    "test": "echo \"Error: no test specified\" && exit 1"
  },
  "repository": {
    "type": "git",
    "url": "https://github.com/isomorphic-javascript-book/thaumoctopus-mimicus.git"
  },
  "keywords": [
    "isomorphic",
    "javascript"
  ],
  "author": "Jason Strimpel",
  "license": "MIT",
  "bugs": {
    "url":
      "https://github.com/isomorphic-javascript-book/thaumoctopus-mimicus/issues"
  },
  "homepage": "https://github.com/isomorphic-javascript-book/thaumoctopus-mimicus"
}
```

Installing the Application Server

In the previous section, we initialized our project and created a *package.json* file that contains the metadata for our project. While this is a necessary process, it does not provide any functionality for our project, nor is it very exciting—so let's get on with the show and have some fun!

All web applications, including isomorphic JavaScript applications, require an application server of sorts. Whether it is simply serving static files or assembling HTML document responses based on service requests and business logic, it is a necessary part and a good place to begin our coding journey together. For our application server we will be using hapi (*http://hapijs.com/*). Installing hapi is a very easy process:

```
$ npm install hapi --save
```

This command not only installs hapi, but also adds a dependency entry to the project's *package.json* file. This is so that when someone (including you) installs your project, all the dependencies required to run the project are installed as well.

Now that we have hapi installed, we can write our first application server. The goal of this first example is to respond with "hello world". In your *index.js* file, enter the code shown in Example 5-2.

Example 5-2. hapi "hello world" example

```
var Hapi = require('hapi');

// Create a server with a host and port
var server = new Hapi.Server();
server.connection({
    host: 'localhost',
    port: 8000
});

// Add the route
server.route({
    method: 'GET',
    path:'/hello',
    handler: function (request, reply) {
        reply('hello world');
    }
});

// Start the server
server.start();
```

To start the application execute `node .` in your terminal, and open your browser to *http://localhost:8000/hello*. If you see "hello world", congratulations! If not, review the previous steps and see if there is anything that you or I might have missed. If all else fails you can try copying this gist (*http://bit.ly/hapihelloworld*) into your *index.js* file.

Writing Next-Generation JavaScript (ES6)

ECMAScript 6 (*http://www.ecmascript.org/*), or ES6, is the latest version of JavaScript, which adds quite a few new features to the language. The specification was approved and published on June 17, 2015. People have mixed opinions about some features, such as the introduction of classes, but overall ES6 has been well received and at the time of writing is being widely adopted by many companies.

ES6 classes are just syntactic sugar on top of prototypal inheritance, like many other nonnative implementations. They were likely added to make the language more appealing to a larger audience by providing a common frame of reference to those coming from classical inheritance languages. We will be utilizing classes throughout the book.

The general consensus in the industry is to begin leveraging the new features afforded by ES6, which are not yet widely supported, now and to compile down to an ECMA-Script version that is widely supported (i.e., ES5). Part of the compilation process is to provide polyfills for the ES6 features missing in the target version. Given this industry trend and readily available compilation support, we will be leveraging ES6 for the rest of the examples in this book. Let's start with updating the code from the last example.

The first thing we want to change is how we are importing our dependency, hapi, in *index.js*. Replace the first line in the *index.js* file with this line:

```
import Hapi from 'hapi';
```

ES6 introduces the concept of a module system to JavaScript, which is a concept that has been missing since its inception. In the absence of a native module interface other patterns have emerged to fill the gap, such as AMD and CommonJS. The `require` syntax from the original *index.js* (Example 5-2) is the CommonJS format.

The reason there is not a native module interface is that when JavaScript was created it was not intended to power applications like it does today. It was intended to be additive and enrich the client experience.

The next change we need to make is to our `server` variable declaration. Replace the second line in the file with:

```
const server = new Hapi.Server();
```

`const` is one of the new variable declarations available in ES6. When a variable is declared using `const`, the reference cannot be changed. For example, if you create an object using `const` and add properties to the object, that will not throw an error because the reference has not changed. However, if you attempted to point the variable to another object, that would result in an error because the reference would change. We use `const` because we don't want to accidentally point our `server` variable to another reference.

`const` is not a value that does not change. It is a constant reference to a value in memory.

Example 5-3 shows what the *index.js* file looks like with these changes in place.

Example 5-3. ES6 updates to hapi "hello world" example

```
import Hapi from 'hapi';

// Create a server with a host and port
const server = new Hapi.Server();
server.connection({
    host: 'localhost',
    port: 8000
});

// Add the route
server.route({
    method: 'GET',
    path:'/hello',
    handler: function (request, reply) {
        reply('hello world');
    }
});

// Start the server
server.start();
```

Now that we have updated *index.js* to use the latest and greatest ES6 syntax, let's try running it. Depending on what version of Node you are running, your results may vary—that is, the browser might not render "hello world". This is because ES6 may not be supported by the version of Node you are running. Fortunately, that is not a problem because there is a compiler that will take our ES6 code and compile it to code that runs in Node 4+.

Compiling from ES6 to ES5

One of the tools mentioned at the beginning of this chapter was Babel (*https://babeljs.io/*), a JavaScript compiler. We will be using Babel throughout the rest of the book to compile our JavaScript, but first we need to install Babel and the ES2015 transformations:

```
$ npm install --save-dev babel-cli babel-preset-es2015
```

Babel Plugin and Presets

By default Babel itself does not do anything. It uses plugins to transform code. The previous command line installed a *preset*, which is a preconfigured plugin or set of plugins for transforming ES6 code to ES5 code so that it will run in legacy browsers and older versions of Node.

Just like the hapi installation command, the previous command will add Babel as a dependency to your *package.json* file. The only difference is that we passed `--save-dev` instead of `--save`, so the dependency will be listed under `devDependencies` in the *package.json* file as opposed to the `dependencies` property. The reason for this is because Babel is not required to run your application, but it is a development requirement. This distinction makes it clear to consumers what dependencies are needed for production vs. development. When your project is installed using the `--production` flag, the Babel CLI will not be installed.

Now that we have successfully installed Babel we can compile *index.js*, but before we do that we should restructure our project a bit.

If we were to leave our project structure as is and compile *index.js*, then we would overwrite our source code—and losing your source code without a backup is not a great experience. The fix for this is to specify an output file for Babel. A common location for a project's distributable is *dist*, and the common directory for source code is *src*. I'm not one for inventing new standards, so let's just stick with those:

```
$ mkdir dist
$ mkdir src
$ mv index.js src/index.js
```

Now that we have a project structure that works well for compiling our source, let's make a change to our *package.json*. The first change is pointing the `main` property to our new distributable by changing the `"main": "index.js,"` line to `"main": "./dist/index.js",`. This informs Node of the new entry point for our application, so that when we execute `node .` it loads the correct script. We are now ready for our first compilation! Enter the following at the command line:

```
$ babel src/index.js --out-file dist/index.js
```

Command Not Found!

If you receive a "Command not found!" error when executing this command, then you might need to specify the path to the executable, `./node_modules/.bin/babel`, or install `babel` globally with `npm install -g babel-cli` instead.

The previous command takes our source, *src/index.js*, compiles it, and creates our distributable, *dist/index.js*. If everything went well then we should be able to start up our server again using `node ..`

Babel and ES6 Features

We've barely scratched the surface of Babel and ES6 in the last few sections. For more information, visit *https://babeljs.io*.

Setting Up a Development Workflow

We now have the ability to compile at will and restart the server via the command line, which is a great accomplishment, but stopping development each time to execute those two commands at the terminal will get old very quickly. Luckily, we are not the first people to have the need to automate repetitive tasks and optimize our workflow, so there are a few different automation choices at our disposal. Naturally we will want to pick the latest and greatest choice, so that our code will remain relevant for the next six months. The most recent addition to the JavaScript build world is Gulp (*http://gulpjs.com/*), a streaming build system in which you create tasks and load plugins from the extensive community-driven ecosystem. These tasks can then be chained together to create your build process. Sounds great, right? Well, let's get started. First we need to install Gulp:

```
$ npm install gulp --save-dev
```

The next thing we need to do is to create a *gulpfile.js* filr at the root of our project and define a default task, as shown in Example 5-4.

Example 5-4. Creating the default Gulp task in gulpfile.js

```
var gulp = require('gulp');

gulp.task('default', function () {
  console.log('default task success!');
});
```

Now that we have Gulp installed and a default task defined, let's run it:

```
$ gulp
[20:00:11] Using gulpfile ./gulpfile.js
[20:00:11] Starting 'default'...
default task success!
[20:00:11] Finished 'default' after 157 µs
```

All absolute paths in the Gulp output have been altered to relative paths (e.g., ./gulpfile.js) so they will fit within the margins of the code blocks. In the output printed to your screen, you will see the absolute path.

Command Not Found!

If you receive a "Command not found!" error when executing the `gulp` command, you might need to specify the path to the executable, `./node_modules/.bin/gulp`, or install gulp globally using `npm install -g gulp` instead.

Success! We have Gulp running. Now let's create a task of substance, like compiling our source. This will require the `gulp-babel` plugin (*https://www.npmjs.com/package/gulp-babel*), which we can install as follows:

```
$ npm install gulp-babel --save-dev
```

In our *gulpfile.js* we now need to modify our default task to handle the compilation. Replace the contents of the file you created earlier with the code shown in Example 5-5.

Example 5-5. Compiling source with gulp-babel

```
var gulp = require('gulp');
var babel = require('gulp-babel');

gulp.task('compile', function () {
  return gulp.src('src/**/*.js')
    .pipe(babel({
      presets: ['es2015']
    }))
    .pipe(gulp.dest('dist'));
});

gulp.task('default', ['compile']);
```

Now let's run Gulp again:

```
$ gulp
[23:55:13] Using gulpfile ./gulpfile.js
[23:55:13] Starting 'compile'...
[23:55:13] Finished 'compile' after 251 ms
[23:55:13] Starting 'default'...
[23:55:13] Finished 'default' after 17 µs
$
```

This is great, but we are no better off than we were before. The only thing we have really done is to reduce the amount of code we have to type at the terminal. In order for the inclusion of Gulp to really add value we need to automate the compilation and server restarting on a source file save.

Watching for source code changes

Gulp has a built-in file watcher, `gulp.watch` (*http://bit.ly/gulpwatch*), that accepts file globs, options, and a task list or callback to be executed when a file changes that matches a glob. This is just what we need to run our Babel task, so let's configure it. Add the following task to *gulpfile.js*:

```
gulp.task('watch', function () {
  gulp.watch('src/**/*.js', ['compile']);
});
```

This should give us just the behavior we are seeking, so let's add it to our default task:

```
gulp.task('default', ['watch', 'compile']);
```

If you run `gulp` in your terminal and make a file change you should now see something similar to the following:

```
$ gulp
[00:04:35] Using gulpfile ./gulpfile.js
[00:04:35] Starting 'watch'...
[00:04:35] Finished 'watch' after 12 ms
[00:04:35] Starting 'compile'...
[00:04:35] Finished 'compile' after 114 ms
[00:04:35] Starting 'default'...
[00:04:35] Finished 'default' after 16 µs
[00:04:39] Starting 'compile'...
[00:04:39] Finished 'compile' after 75 ms
```

This is really nice because now we don't have to run our compile command every time we make a source code change. Now we just need to get the server to restart automatically.

Restarting the server on distribution changes

To watch for changes to the distribution file, *dist/index.js*, we will be using the gulp-nodemon (*https://www.npmjs.com/package/gulp-nodemon*) plugin, which wraps nodemon (*http://nodemon.io/*). nodemon is a utility that watches for changes and automatically restarts your server when changes are made. Before we can begin leveraging gulp-nodemon, we have to install it:

```
$ npm install gulp-nodemon --save-dev
```

Next we need to install run-sequence:

```
$ npm install run-sequence --save-dev
```

This will run a sequence of Gulp tasks in a specified order. This is necessary because we need to ensure that our distributable exists before we try to start the server.

Now we need to code the imperative bits in our *gulpfile.js* file that instruct gulp-nodemon when to restart the server and include run-sequence. Add the following lines to the file:

```
var nodemon = require('gulp-nodemon');
var sequence = require('run-sequence');

gulp.task('start', function () {
  nodemon({
    watch: 'dist',
    script: 'dist/index.js',
    ext: 'js',
    env: { 'NODE_ENV': 'development' }
  });
});
```

Lastly, we need to add our new nodemon task to our default task and use run-sequence to specify the task execution order:

```
gulp.task('default', function (callback) {
  sequence(['compile', 'watch'], 'start', callback);
});
```

Now when you run the default task and make a source code change you should see something similar to the following:

```
$ gulp
[16:51:43] Using gulpfile ./gulpfile.js
[16:51:43] Starting 'default'...
[16:51:43] Starting 'compile'...
[16:51:43] Starting 'watch'...
[16:51:43] Finished 'watch' after 5.04 ms
[16:51:44] Finished 'compile' after 57 ms
[16:51:44] Starting 'start'...
[16:51:44] Finished 'start' after 849 µs
[16:51:44] Finished 'default' after 59 ms
[16:51:44] [nodemon] v1.4.0
[16:51:44] [nodemon] to restart at any time, enter `rs`
[16:51:44] [nodemon] watching: ./dist/**/*
[16:51:44] [nodemon] starting `node dist/index.js`
[16:51:47] Starting 'compile'...
[16:51:47] Finished 'compile' after 19 ms
[16:51:48] [nodemon] restarting due to changes...
[16:51:48] [nodemon] starting `node dist/index.js`
```

Your completed *gulpfile.js* should look like Example 5-6.

Example 5-6. Completed gulpfile.js

```
var gulp = require('gulp');
var babel = require('gulp-babel');
var nodemon = require('gulp-nodemon');
```

```
var sequence = require('run-sequence');

gulp.task('compile', function () {
  return gulp.src('src/**/*.js')
    .pipe(babel({
      presets: ['es2015']
    }))
    .pipe(gulp.dest('dist'));
});

gulp.task('watch', function () {
  gulp.watch('src/**/*.js', ['compile']);
});

gulp.task('start', function () {
  nodemon({
    watch: 'dist',
    script: 'dist/index.js',
    ext: 'js',
    env: { 'NODE_ENV': 'development' }
  });
});

gulp.task('default', function (callback) {
  sequence(['compile', 'watch'], 'start', callback);
});
```

Summary

We covered quite a bit of material in this chapter, from installing Node to optimizing our development workflow for our first hapi application server, including the usage of ES6. All of this was in preparation for modern JavaScript application development. This knowledge also doubles as the foundation for the working example application we will begin building in Chapter 6.

Completed Code Examples

You can install the completed code examples from this chapter by executing npm install thaumoctopus-mimicus@"0.1.x" in your terminal.

Serving Our First HTML Document

Jason Strimpel

When creating an isomorphic JavaScript framework or application, most people begin with the client and then attempt to fit their solution to the server. This is likely because they began with a client-side application and later realized that they needed some of the benefits that an isomorphic application provides, such as an optimized page load. The problem with this approach is that client implementations are typically deeply linked to the browser environment, which makes transferring the application to the server a complicated process. This is not to say that starting from the server makes us impervious to environment-specific issues, but it does ensure that we begin from a request/reply lifecycle mindset, which is required by the server. And, the real advantage we have is that we do not have an investment in an existing code base, so we get to start with a clean slate!

Serving an HTML Template

Before we build any abstractions or define an API, let's start with serving an HTML document based on a template, so we can familiarize ourselves with the server request/reply lifecycle. For this example and the rest that follow we will be using Nunjucks (*https://mozilla.github.io/nunjucks/*) by Mozilla (*https://www.mozilla.org*), which you can install as follows:

```
$ npm install nunjucks -save
```

Now that we have Nunjucks installed we can create a template, *src/index.html*, with the contents shown in Example 6-1.

Example 6-1. Nunjucks HTML document template

```
<head>
  <meta charset="utf-8">
  <title>
    And the man in the suit has just bought a new car
    From the profit he's made on your dreams
  </title>
</head>
<body>
  <p>hello {{fname}} {{lname}}</p>
</body>
</html>
```

Nunjucks uses double curly braces to render variables from the template context. Next, let's modify *./src/index.js* to return the compiled template with a first and last name when a user opens *localhost:8000/hello+* in the browser. Edit the file so it matches the version shown in Example 6-2.

Example 6-2. Serving an HTML document (./src/index.js)

```
import Hapi from 'hapi';
import nunjucks from 'nunjucks';

// configure nunjucks to read from the dist directory
nunjucks.configure('./dist');

// create a server with a host and port
const server = new Hapi.Server();
server.connection({
  host: 'localhost',
  port: 8000
});

// add the route
server.route({
  method: 'GET',
  path:'/hello',
  handler: function (request, reply) {
    // read template and compile using context object
    nunjucks.render('index.html', {
      fname: 'Rick', lname: 'Sanchez'
    }, function (err, html) {
      // reply with HTML response
      reply(html);
    });
  }
});

// start the server
server.start();
```

We made quite a few changes to our example from Chapter 5. Let's break these down item by item and discuss them. The first thing we did was import nunjucks. Next, we configured nunjucks (*https://mozilla.github.io/nunjucks/api.html#configure*) to read from the *./dist* directory. Finally, we used nunjucks to read our template, *./dist/ index.html*, compile it using our context variable { fname: Rick, lname: San chez }, and then return an HTML string as the reply from our server.

This code looks great, but if you run gulp in the terminal and try to open *localhost: 8000/hello* in a browser it will return an empty <body>. So why doesn't it work? If you remember, we created our template in *./src*, but we configured nunjucks to read from *./dist* (which is what we want because *./dist* contains our application distribution and *./src* contains our application source). So how do we fix this? We need to update our build to copy our template. Modify *gulpfile.js*, adding a copy task and editing the watch task and the default task as shown in Example 6-3.

Example 6-3. Copying the template from source to distribution (gulpfile.js)

```
// previous code omitted for brevity

gulp.task('copy', function () {
  return gulp.src('src/**/*.html')
    .pipe(gulp.dest('dist'));
});

gulp.task('watch', function () {
  gulp.watch('src/**/*.js', ['compile']);
  gulp.watch('src/**/*.html', ['copy']);
});

// previous code omitted for brevity

gulp.task('default', function (callback) {
  sequence(['compile', 'watch', 'copy'], 'start', callback);
});
```

Now if we run gulp in the terminal and open the browser to *localhost:8000/hello* we should see "hello Rick Sanchez". Success!

This is pretty cool, but not very dynamic. What if we want to change the first and the last name in the body response? We need to pass parameters to the server, similar (conceptually) to the way we pass arguments to a function.

Working with Path and Query Parameters

Often, an application needs to serve dynamic content. Path and query parameters, and sometimes a session cookie, drive the selection of this content by the server. In the previous section the first and last name values for our hello message were hardcoded in the route handler, but there is no reason why the values could not be determined by path parameters. In order to pass path parameters to our route handler, we need to update the `path` property of our route as shown in Example 6-4.

Example 6-4. Adding path parameters in ./src/index.js

```
server.route({
  method: 'GET',
  path:'/hello/{fname}/{lname}',
  handler: function (request, reply) {
    // read template and compile using context object
    nunjucks.render('index.html', {
      fname: 'Rick', lname: 'Sanchez'
    }, function (err, html) {
      // reply with HTML response
      reply(html);
    });
  }
});
```

With this change, the route will now match URIs like *localhost:8000/hello/morty/smith* and *localhost:8000/hello/jerry/smith*. The new values in these URI paths are path parameters (*http://hapijs.com/api#path-parameters*) and will be part of the request object: *request.params.fname* and *request.params.lname*. These values can then be passed to the template context, as shown in Example 6-5.

Example 6-5. Accessing path parameters

```
server.route({
  method: 'GET',
  path:'/hello/{fname}/{lname}',
  handler: function (request, reply) {
    // read template and compile using context object
    nunjucks.render('index.html', {
      fname: request.params.fname,
      laname: request.params.lname
    }, function (err, html) {
      // reply with HTML response
      reply(html);
    });
  }
});
```

If you load *localhost:8000/hello/jerry/smith* in your browser you should now see path parameters in the response body.

Another way to pass values via the URI is using query parameters (*https://en.wikipe dia.org/wiki/Query_string*), as in *localhost:8000/hello?fname=morty&lname=smith* and *localhost:8000/hello?fname=jerry&lname=smith*. To enable the use of query parameters, change the route to match Example 6-6.

Example 6-6. Accessing query parameters

```
server.route({
  method: 'GET',
  path:'/hello',
  handler: function (request, reply) {
    // read template and compile using context object
    nunjucks.render('index.html', {
      fname: request.query.fname,
      laname: request.query.lname
    }, function (err, html) {
      // reply with HTML response
      reply(html);
    });
  }
});
```

Those are two different ways for getting dynamic values to a route that can be used to drive the selection of dynamic content. You can also use both of these options and provide sensible defaults to create a more flexible route handler, as shown in Example 6-7.

Example 6-7. Accessing path and query parameters

```
function getName(request) {
  // default values
  let name = {
    fname: 'Rick',
    lname: 'Sanchez'
  };
  // split path params
  let nameParts = request.params.name ? request.params.name.split('/') : [];

  // order of precedence
  // 1. path param
  // 2. query param
  // 3. default value
  name.fname = (nameParts[0] || request.query.fname) ||
    name.fname;
  name.lname = (nameParts[1] || request.query.lname) ||
    name.lname;

  return name;
}

// add the route
server.route({
```

```
    method: 'GET',
    path:'/hello/{name*}',
    handler: function (request, reply) {
      // read template and compile using context object
      nunjucks.render('index.html', getName(request), function (err, html) {
        // reply with HTML response
        reply(html);
      });
    }
});
```

These examples were intentionally contrived for the sake of simplicity so we could focus on the concepts, but in the real world path and query parameters are often used to make service calls or query a database.

 In Chapter 8 we will cover routes in more detail, including the creation of an isomorphic router using call (*https://github.com/hapijs/call*), the HTTP router that is used by hapi.

Summary

In this chapter we learned how to serve an HTML document based on a template that rendered dynamic content. We also became more familiar with the request/reply lifecycle and some of its properties, such as `request.params` and `request.query`. This knowledge will be used throughout the rest of this part of the book as we build out our application.

 Completed Code Examples

You can install the completed code examples from this chapter by executing `npm install thaumoctopus-mimicus@"0.2.x"` in your terminal.

CHAPTER 7

Architecting Our Application

Jason Strimpel

If you have been working as a frontend developer for long enough, you probably remember a time before the proliferation of the MV* libraries that now both complicate and improve web development. If you have been in the industry even longer, you can probably recall the days before jQuery. For me, those memories are colored by the frustration of attempting to debug a 4,000-line JavaScript file that was a comprised of miscellaneous functions and "classes," which made references to other 4,000-line JavaScript files. Even if you cannot remember those days of yore, you have probably encountered similar difficult-to-follow, frustrating code.

Most often, the source of the frustration is a lack of form and structure, the building blocks of a good architecture. As James Coplien and Gertrud Bjørnvig put it in *Lean Architecture: For Agile Software Development* (Wiley), we can "think of form as being the essential shape or arrangement of a thing without regard to what it is made of, and of structure as the reification of form." In our case an example of form is an `Application` class that accepts route definitions. An example of structure is the ES6 module format that uses `export` and `import`.

Another overly utilized component of architecture is *abstraction*. The key to properly utilizing abstraction is to use it only when necessary, because it hides details, which makes code more difficult to follow and read. Otherwise, you end up with numerous wrapper functions with convoluted implementations that become very brittle over time. We will be leveraging abstractions to solve a few commonly encountered problems when developing isomorphic JavaScript applications, such as getting and setting cookies, but it's important not to go overboard.

Placing emphasis on form and structure early on reduces the likelihood of unexpected outcomes and improves the maintainability of our code. Along with a healthy skepticism of abstractions, this will ensure our application stands the industry test of time (five years).

Understanding the Problem

We already know that we are creating an isomorphic JavaScript application, but what does that mean in terms of architecture? In order to answer that question we must first define the problem we're aiming to solve. Our goal is to efficiently serve an SEO-compliant user interface in a web browser. The efficiency aspect of our goal relates to running the application on both client and server, so that it can take advantage of the benefits of both environments. Since it will have to run on the client and the server, we must start thinking in terms of abstracting the environments without introducing unnecessary complexities. So where do we begin? From the beginning of the user request with the innovation that connects us all (*http://bit.ly/thepowerofconnection*): the URL.

Responding to User Requests

The URL is what connects a user to your application. Your application uses the URL to map to specific resources that are returned by your application logic. This is what makes the Web work, and what makes it a fitting place to start adding structure to our application. In the examples from the previous chapters we used the hapi `server.route` API for adding routes to our application that respond to user requests. This approach works well for applications that only run on the server and leverage hapi as their application server. But in our case we want our application to run on the client in addition to the server, so referencing hapi directly will not suffice. Additionally, direct references to hapi throughout your application code tightly couple your code to hapi, making it difficult to swap it out later if desired or necessary.

Abstractions

Sometimes people take abstractions too far. For instance, creating an API wrapper around a library in your application or framework simply to make replacing a library in the future easier is not a good reason. It is not a wise investment of time because you are solving for a problem that has not yet occurred and may never occur. Abstractions should provide an immediate or imminent value. Good form and structure should be used to help ensure longevity of software in favor of numerous, premature abstractions.

Creating the Application Class

The first step to providing structure when responding to user requests is to create an application class that can be reused across your applications. The purpose of this class is to reduce boilerplate and provide an interface that will eventually be used on both the client and the server.

In the case of defining user routes we need an interface that will allow our application's *./src/index.js* file to do something like Example 7-1.

Example 7-1. Using an Application class

```
import Hapi from 'hapi';
import nunjucks from 'nunjucks';
import Application from './lib';

// configure nunjucks to read from the dist directory
nunjucks.configure('./dist');

// create a server with a host and port
const server = new Hapi.Server();
server.connection({
  host: 'localhost',
  port: 8000
});

function getName(request) {
  // function body omitted for brevity
}

const application = new Application({
  // responds to http://localhost:8000/
  '/': function (request, reply) {
    // read template and compile using context object
    nunjucks.render('index.html', getName(request), function (err, html) {
      // reply with HTML response
      reply(html);
    });
  }
}, {
  server: server
});

application.start();
```

 Earlier, we spoke about making the correct abstractions. Abstracting the server instantiation details in this case did not provide a benefit, so we left them intact. In the future these details could be moved to a separate module, if the configuration grows and makes the application file difficult to follow or we are registering numerous hapi plugins (*http://hapijs.com/plugins*).

If your first reaction to Example 7-1 was "I don't see the benefit," don't worry; that is the correct reaction! We'd be wrong to do nothing more than implement an application class to support this code, because this would only encapsulate the implementation details without providing any benefits. In our case we are providing a foundation that we will progressively build upon, and the benefits will reveal themselves over the course of Part II. Now that we have cleared that up, let's get to the implementation. We define our `Application` class in *./src/lib/index.js*, as shown in Example 7-2.

Example 7-2. Application class

```
export default class Application {

  constructor(routes, options) {
    this.server = options.server;
    this.registerRoutes(routes);
  }

  registerRoutes(routes) {
    for (let path in routes) {
      this.addRoute(path, routes[path]);
    }
  }

  addRoute(path, handler) {
    this.server.route({
      path: path,
      method: 'GET',
      handler: handler
    });
  }

  start() {
    this.server.start();
  }

}
```

We now have a basic application façade that we will eventually amend with a client implementation. This is a great start, but as noted earlier we haven't added any real benefit to our application other than preparing it for transport to the client later. In order to add some value at this stage we need to reduce some of the boilerplate code associated with route definitions and add some more structure to how we are responding to user requests.

Creating a Controller

We can further improve the structure and reduce boilerplate by creating a common way to respond to URLs. In order to do that we need to create an interface that application developers can code against. As with the application structure we set up in Example 7-2, there will be little if any benefit at this point, within the context of current example, but we will build on this foundation.

In Struts, Ruby on Rails, ASP.Net, etc., controllers have action methods that are called by the framework. The controllers and actions are mapped to paths in a route table. These action methods contain the business logic for processing incoming requests and responding accordingly. In our case we want to respond with a user interface, which will be a payload of HTML. Knowing that, let's begin by defining a basic interface, as shown in Example 7-3 (*./src/lib/controller.js*).

Example 7-3. Controller class

```
export default class Controller {

  constructor(context) {
    this.context = context;
  }

  index(application, request, reply, callback) {
    callback(null);
  }

  toString(callback) {
    callback(null, 'success');
  }

}
```

The `constructor` method creates an instance of the `Controller` class. The argument `context` contains metadata related to the route, such as path and query parameters. This data will be useful on the client when a controller instance persists after the action has replied to the request.

The `index` method is the default action for a controller instance, which accepts four arguments:

1. `application` is a reference to the application that defined the route. This will be useful in the future for accessing application-level methods and properties.

2. `request` is the hapi `request` object. This can be used for request-level actions such as reading header or cookie values. In the future this object will be normalized, so that it functions the same across the client and the server.

3. `reply` is the hapi `reply` object. This can be used to redirect a request, as in `reply.redirect(some/url)`. In the future this object will be normalized, so that it functions the same across the client and the server.

4. `callback` is a Node-style callback (*http://bit.ly/nodestylecallback*) for asynchronous control flow. If the first parameter is `null`, the handler that called the action method will proceed forward in the request/reply lifecycle. If it is an `Error` (*http://bit.ly/errorobject*), the application responds with an error (we will cover error responses in more detail later).

`toString` is the method that will be called by the application framework after the action method `callback` has been executed without erring. The second parameter of a successful `callback` should be the string to be rendered.

Constructing a Controller Instance

Now that we have defined a contract for responding to resource requests, we can move more of the logic associated with defining routes to our application framework. If you remember, our *./src/index.js* still contains route definitions with inline functions (see Example 7-4).

Example 7-4. Inline route handler

```
const application = new Application({
  // responds to http://localhost:8000/
  '/': function (request, reply) {
    // read template and compile using context object
    nunjucks.render('index.html', getName(request), function (err, html) {
      // reply with HTML response
      reply(html);
    });
  }
}, {
  server: server
});
```

Now that we have a base controller this can be transformed to the version in Example 7-5.

Example 7-5. Using the Controller class

```
import Hapi from 'hapi';
import Application from './lib';
import Controller from './lib/controller'

const server = new Hapi.Server();
server.connection({
  host: 'localhost',
  port: 8000
});

const application = new Application({
```

```
  '/': Controller
}, {
  server: server
});

application.start();
```

That looks a lot better. We successfully removed the rendering and response implementation details, making our application much easier to read. At a glance we can now quickly discern that `Controller` will be responding to *http://localhost:8000/*. This is a true work of art. The downside is that it will not work! We need to implement code in *src/lib/index.js* that will create an instance that responds via a route handler. The change we need to make is to update our `Application` class's `addRoute` method, as shown in Example 7-6, to create a handler that creates a controller instance and follows the lifecycle contract of the controller.

Example 7-6. Application class addRoute method

```
addRoute(path, Controller) {
  this.server.route({
    path: path,
    method: 'GET',
    handler: (request, reply) => {
      const controller = new Controller({
        query: request.query,
        params: request.params
      });

      controller.index(this, request, reply, (err) => {
        if (err) {
          return reply(err);
        }

        controller.toString((err, html) => {
          if (err) {
            return reply(err);
          }

          reply(html);
        });
      });
    }
  });
}
```

Some new syntax is introduced in this example that might be a bit confusing if you are not familiar with these constructs: arrow functions (*http://bit.ly/arrowfunctions*). The purpose of using arrow functions in this case is to lexically bind this, so that we do not have to create variables such as self or that, or explicitly bind (*http://bit.ly/bindfunction*) functions to set the context.

If you open up *http://localhost:8000/* in your browser you should see "success," which is the expected result, but not the desired result.

Extending the Controller

In our previous route handler we passed the file contexts of *./src/index.html* to Nunjucks, compiled it, provided a context object, and finally replied with string that was the result of the template function. Let's take a look at what this would look like in our new world. Example 7-7 shows the extended Controller class (*./src/HelloController.js*).

Example 7-7. Extending the base Controller

```
import Controller from './lib/controller';
import nunjucks from 'nunjucks';

// configure nunjucks to read from the dist directory
nunjucks.configure('./dist');

function getName(context) {
  // function body omitted for brevity
}

export default class HelloController extends Controller {

  toString(callback) {
    // read template and compile using context object
    nunjucks.render('index.html', getName(this.context), (err, html) => {
      if (err) {
        return callback(err, null);
      }
      callback(null, html);
    });
  }

}
```

This functions essentially the same as Example 7-4, but we have encapsulated the logic responsible for replying to *http://localhost:8000/* in our controller. If we wanted, we could make this the base controller for the application and create some conventions for resolving to a template file based on the route. For instance, we could make the `request.uri` part of the `context` object and use `request.uri.path` to locate the template in a corresponding directory in *./dist*. We are not going to implement this convention-based approach, but the point is that you can put common application-specific code in a base controller to promote reuse.

Next we need to update *./src/index.js* to use our new controller and update the route path to accept optional path parameters, as seen in Example 7-8.

Example 7-8. Accepting path parameters

```
import Hapi from 'hapi';
import Application from './lib';
import HelloController from './hello-controller';

const server = new Hapi.Server();
server.connection({
  host: 'localhost',
  port: 8000
});

const application = new Application({
  '/hello/{name*}': HelloController
}, {
  server: server
});

application.start();
```

If you open up *http://localhost:8000/* in your browser you should now see the expected hello message.

Improving the Response Flow

In preparation for porting the code to the client, there is one last implementation that we are going to change. Instead of the controller reading and creating the HTML response, we are going to create an API for returning a page template in which we can inject the results from the controller's `toString` callback. The new version of *./src/HelloController.js* can be seen in Example 7-9.

Example 7-9. Creating an inline template

```
import Controller from './lib/controller';
import nunjucks from 'nunjucks';

function getName(context) {
  // function body omitted for brevity
}
```

```
export default class HelloController extends Controller {

  toString(callback) {
    nunjucks.renderString('<p>hello  </p>', getName(this.context), (err, html) => {
      if (err) {
        return callback(err, null);
      }
      callback(null, html);
    });
  }

}
```

The reason we are doing this is so that when our application transitions to an SPA on the client our routes will only return the HTML for a route as opposed to an entire document. This also has certain performance advantages. For example, on the server we could potentially limit the amount of file system I/O. On the client we could create a layout that has a header and footer that don't rerender when navigating or that doesn't require us to reparse <script> tags. From the application's perspective, these are the changes that we will make to ./src/index.js (Example 7-10).

Example 7-10. Defining the application HTML document

```
import Hapi from 'hapi';
import Application from './lib';
import HelloController from './hello-controller';
import nunjucks from 'nunjucks';

// configure nunjucks to read from the dist directory
nunjucks.configure('./dist');

const server = new Hapi.Server();
server.connection({
  host: 'localhost',
  port: 8000
});

const application = new Application({
  '/hello/{name*}': HelloController
}, {
  server: server,
  document: function (application, controller, request, reply, body, callback) {
    nunjucks.render('./index.html', { body: body }, (err, html) => {
      if (err) {
        return callback(err, null);
      }
      callback(null, html);
    });
  }
});
```

```
application.start();
```

These changes will allow us to inject a controller's toString callback value, the body
argument, into a page template without imposing a technology choice on the framework. Let's implement the application framework changes now. The final version of
the addRoute method is shown in Example 7-11.

Example 7-11. Replying to a resource request (Application class addRoute method)

```
addRoute(path, Controller) {
  this.server.route({
    path: path,
    method: 'GET',
    handler: (request, reply) => {
      const controller = new Controller({
        query: request.query,
        params: request.params
      });

      controller.index(this, request, reply, (err) => {
        if (err) {
          return reply(err);
        }

        controller.toString((err, html) => {
          if (err) {
            return reply(err);
          }

          this.document(this, controller, request, reply, html,
            function (err, html) {
            if (err) {
              return reply(err);
            }

            reply(html);
          });
        });
      });
    }
  });
}
```

Now the application framework is responsible for composing the HTML document
response, but the implementation details of the HTML string construction are left up
to the application developer. The final change we need to make is to our template, as
seen in Example 7-12 (*./src/index.html*).

Example 7-12. Adding an outlet for the document body

```
<head>
  <meta charset="utf-8">
  <title>
    And the man in the suit has just bought a new car
    From the profit he's made on your dreams
  </title>
</head>
<body>
  {{body}}
</body>
</html>
```

If we open the browser to *http://localhost:8000/* we should see the expected "hello world" message.

There is an ES6 template string API (*http://bit.ly/templateliterals*) that works well for embedding expressions into strings. The reason we are not using it is because we are reading from the filesystem. Converting the file contents string into a template string would require the use of eval (e.g., eval(*templateStr*);), which presents some security risks.

Figure 7-1 illustrates the completed request/reply lifecycle.

Summary

In this chapter we created a solid foundation upon which we can build. We achieved this by adding form and structure to our application. We defined a clear contract between the application and the framework for responding to resource requests. These deliberate actions will allow us to easily swap out pieces in the future, enabling us to easily respond to change wholesale or gradually as we experiment with new technologies. More importantly, this will help ensure stability. In the next chapter the real fun begins, as we start porting our application and framework to the client!

Completed Code Examples

You can install the completed code examples from this chapter by executing npm install thaumoctopus-mimicus@"0.3.x" in your terminal.

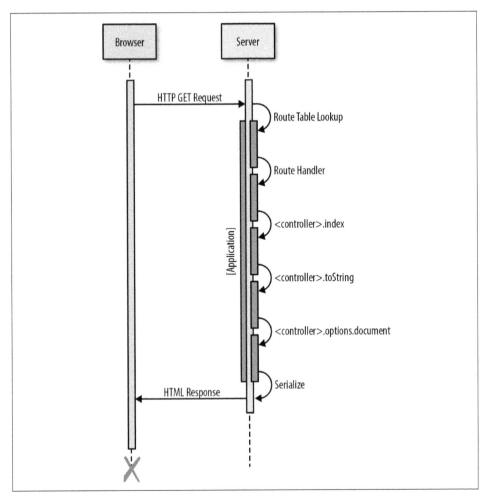

Figure 7-1. Request/reply lifecycle

CHAPTER 8

Transporting the Application to the Client

Jason Strimpel

Up until now our efforts have been focused on building a solid foundation for our application. In this chapter we will begin to reap the benefits of our careful planning as we update our server-only application to run on the client. If we have done our job well, this should be a fairly easy task; once we are done, we will have the core of a fully functioning isomorphic JavaScript application. However, before we begin the process of porting our application to the client, we need to make some additions to our build process and modify the structure of the application.

Bundling Our Application for the Client

This first thing we need to do in order to run our application on the client is to create an application bundle file that contains our entire application source. This file will be included by *./src/index.html*, which is served as the first page response from the server.

If your application is large you may want to split it up into multiple bundles to improve the initial page load experience.

Selecting a Bundling Library

There are two primary bundling libraries currently being leveraged by the community to create client application bundles: Browserify (*http://browserify.org/*) and Webpack (*http://webpack.github.io/*).

Asynchronous Module Definition (AMD)

There is a third bundling library, the RequireJS Optimizer (*http://requirejs.org/docs/optimization.html*), that leverages RequireJS, which implements the AMD pattern (*https://github.com/amdjs/amdjs-api/blob/master/AMD.md*): an API specifies a mechanism for defining modules such that the module and its dependencies can be asynchronously loaded. However, the industry has been moving toward more synchronous module loading patterns such as CommonJS (*http://wiki.commonjs.org/wiki/CommonJS*), so we will not be covering it.

Browserify was created to allow you to develop your client applications as if you were writing a Node application by using the Node `require` syntax to include dependencies. It also has client versions of some core Node libraries, so that you can include them and make use of their APIs as you would on the server.

Webpack was created to bundle all resource types—CSS, AMD, SASS, images, CoffeeScript, etc.—for the client. It has some built-in plugins and supports the concept of code splitting, which allows you to easily split your application into multiple files so that you do not have to load the entire application at once.

Both libraries are excellent choices, and you can accomplish the same results with either. Their approaches are just a bit different. We'll be using Browserify because it will not require complex configuration for our use case, which makes it slightly easier to get started.

Creating Our Bundle Task

In this section we will create our first application bundle for the client. The bundle task itself is extremely easy to execute, but it requires some initial setup. The first step in the process is to install some new build tools, starting with the `browserify` module:

```
$ npm install browserify --save-dev
```

Later in the process we will use `browserify` to create a task in *gulpfile.js* that builds our application bundle. We also need to install the `babelify` module:

```
$ npm install babelify --save-dev
```

Babelify (*https://github.com/babel/babelify*) is a Browserify transform (*https://github.com/substack/browserify-handbook#transforms*) that transforms our source from ES6 to ES5, just like our `compile` task. This seems a bit redundant, but if we ever need to add other transforms in the future—e.g., `brfs` (*https://github.com/substack/brfs*)—then it will be necessary to bundle from source and use a transformer as opposed to bundling from the already compiled distribution. We will be piping a conventional text stream from Browserify to Gulp, so we need to install `vinyl-source-stream` as well:

```
$ npm install vinyl-source-stream --save-dev
```

Node Streams

A stream (*https://nodejs.org/api/stream.html*) is an abstract interface implemented by various objects in Node. For example, a request to an HTTP server is a stream, as is `stdout`. Streams are readable, writable, or both. All streams are instances of EventEmitter.

Next we need to provide some instructions to Browserify, so that it will bundle up client-specific implementations when necessary. Adding the `browser` property to the *package.json* file, as shown here:

```
{
  "browser": {
    "./src/index.js": "./src/index.client.js"
  }
}
```

lets Browserify know that when it encounters a specific file, *./src/index.js*, it should package a different file, *.src/index.client.js*, which contains an implementation for the client. This might seem a bit counterintuitive since we are writing code that is supposed to run on the client and the server, but there are times when we don't really have an option (e.g., we can't run a hapi server on the client). The key is to limit and isolate these patches of code to pieces that change infrequently, so that our daily development isn't greatly impacted by context switching between environments.

The final step is to update our *gulpfile.js* file. First we need to include our newly installed modules:

```
var browserify = require('browserify');
var source = require('vinyl-source-stream');
```

Next we need to create our new `bundle` task:

```
gulp.task('bundle', function () {
  var b = browserify({
    entries: 'src/index.js',
    debug: true
  })
  .transform('babelify', { presets: ['es2015'] });

  return b.bundle()
    .pipe(source('build/application.js'))
    .pipe(gulp.dest('dist'));
});
```

This task will run *./src/index.client.js* through `browserify` tracing any dependencies found. It creates a single file, which gets written to *./dist/build/application.js*. Next, we will add the `bundle` task to our default task:

```
gulp.task('default', function (callback) {
  sequence(['compile', 'watch', 'copy', 'bundle'], 'start', callback);
});
```

Finally, we need to update our `watch` task so that the bundle is written when we make a source code change:

```
gulp.task('watch', function () {
  gulp.watch('src/**/*.js', ['compile', 'bundle'])
  gulp.watch('src/**/*.html', ['copy']);
});
```

That's it! We are now ready to create our bundle—but first we need to add the client implementation that we specified in our *package.json*.

Adding Our Client Implementation

In *./src/index.js*, the entry point for our application, we instantiate a hapi server. This is just the kind of environment-specific code that we need to ensure doesn't make it to the client. We already took a look at how to specify different implementations for the client and the server in the previous section by leveraging the `browser` property in the *package.json* file, where we defined a file, *./src/index.client.js*, to substitute for *./src/index.js*. Our first pass on this will simply be to print "hello browser" to the console:

```
console.log('hello browser');
```

Now we need to include a link to the file in our application template *./src/index.html*, as shown in Example 8-1.

Example 8-1. Including the application bundle in the page template

```
<html>
  <head>
    <meta charset="utf-8">
    <title>
      And the man in the suit has just bought a new car
      From the profit he's made on your dreams
    </title>
  </head>
  <body>
    {{body}}
  </body>
  <script type="text/javascript" src={{application}}></script>
</html>
```

We will pass the path to the application bundle file as a property of the rendering context in *./src/index.js*, as illustrated in Example 8-2.

Example 8-2. Adding the bundle path to the template rendering context

```
const APP_FILE_PATH = '/application.js';
const application = new Application({
  '/hello/{name*}': HelloController
}, {
  server: server,
  document: function (application, controller, request, reply, body, callback) {
    nunjucks.render('./index.html', {
      body: body,
      application: APP_FILE_PATH
    }, (err, html) => {
      if (err) {
        return callback(err, null);
      }
      callback(null, html);
    });
  }
});
```

Finally, we need to add a route to our server in *./src/index.js* that serves our bundle:

```
server.route({
  method: 'GET',
  path: APP_FILE_PATH,
  handler: (request, reply) => {
    reply.file('dist/build/application.js');
  }
});
```

Now when we execute our default Gulp task at the terminal and open *http://localhost: 8000/* in a browser we should see the same result, as before, but if we open the console in the browser we should see "hello browser". If you see this message, then congratulations—you just served your first application bundle! While this example is trivial, the steps and understanding required to set it up will benefit us as we proceed with making our application isomorphic.

Responding to User Requests

In the previous chapter we identified the URL as the mechanism through which a user makes requests of our application. We used this cornerstone of the Web as the starting point for building our application framework on the server. We took incoming requests and mapped them to a route handler that executed a controller action. This was used to construct a response for the client request. This request/response lifecycle constitutes the core of our application framework, and we must ensure that the client supports the contracts defined by this lifecycle so that our application code executes in a predictable manner.

The first part of this contract is that we need to respond to the request the user makes (i.e., the URL). On the server this is an HTTP request. On the client we will not have an HTTP request object, but we still want to execute the application code on the client in order to take advantage of the SPA model's performance benefits. On the client we will likely be responding to a user clicking on a link, which updates the URL in the browser's address bar. It is this changing of the URL that we must respond to on the client, like we respond to an HTTP request on the server. In order to execute our request/reply lifecycle on the client, we essentially want to hijack these clicks that would normally change the URL and make an HTTP request for an HTML document, causing a full page load. We also want to ensure that we do not break the browser history, so that when a user navigates forward or backward using the browser this works as expected. Fortunately, there is already a native interface, the History API (*http://bit.ly/apihist*), that we can utilize.

Leveraging the History API

Before the History API existed, SPAs used hash fragments (*https://en.wikipedia.org/ wiki/Fragment_identifier*) as a workaround for routing to "pages" within an application on the client. Hash fragment changes create new entries in the browser history without reloading the page, but SEO is not supported because hash fragments are not sent to the server as part of an HTTP request. The reason they are not sent is because they were designed to link to a position in a document. The History API was created to ensure that URLs still serve their intended purpose—identifying unique resources —within SPAs and that their contents are properly indexed by search engines.

The History API is very simple. There is a stack onto which you can push a state object, title, and URL. For our purposes, mapping URLs to routes in a routing table, we are only concerned with two methods and one event:

History.replaceState

> This method updates the most recent entry on the history stack. This is useful for adding a state object to a server-rendered page.

History.pushState

> This method pushes a state object, optional title, and optional URL onto the stack. This is helpful for storing URL state that can be used to improve the responsiveness of client-side navigations. For example, all the data required to render a page could be stored in the state object, which could be used to short-circuit network requests for data when navigating to previously rendered pages.

PopStateEvent

This event is fired when the active history entry changes, such as when the user clicks the browser's back button. Listening for this event can be used to trigger client-side navigations to a route.

These methods and this event will be used to trigger route requests for unique resources via URLs on the client, just as an HTTP GET request is used on the server.

Responding to and Calling the History API

In this section we will update our application core to work with the History API to facilitate client-side routing. Before we implement this, though, a word of caution. In this section we will be creating our first real abstraction. I typically avoid abstractions like the plague because they hide details, which obfuscates meaning, making code more difficult to follow and brittle—as James Coplien says, "Abstraction is evil." However, sometimes abstractions are necessary, which is true in this case because we cannot run a server on the client.

In "Adding Our Client Implementation" on page 70 we created a client bundle that logged "hello browser". The entry point for this bundle was *./src/index.js*, which we configured in our *package.json* to point to the client implementation, *./src/index.client.js*, of *./src/index.js*, which is the entry point for the server. This server entry imports the application core, *./src/lib/index.js*, and starts the application. We need to follow the same form for the client implementation, as shown in Example 8-3.

Example 8-3. Client bundle entry point

```
import Application from './lib';
import HelloController from './HelloController';

const application = new Application({
  '/hello/{name*}': HelloController
}, {
  // query selector for the element in which
  // the controller response should be injected
  target: 'body'
});

application.start();
```

 For the time being we are going to focus simply on working with the History API and not on code reuse. We will find the reuse points after we have completed the initial client implementation. Also, in this section we will be ignoring route definitions, which will be covered in "Routing on the Client" on page 77.

Next we need implement the client `Application` class that will encapsulate the History API code—but first we need to add a new property to our `package.json` browser field:

```
{
  "browser": {
    "./src/index.js": "./src/index.client.js",
    "./src/lib/index.js": "./src/lib/index.client.js"
  }
}
```

This will instruct Browserify to use *./src/lib/index.client.js* when bundling. Now we can start to fill in our `Application` class in *./src/lib/index.client.js*, as seen in Example 8-4.

Example 8-4. Application class stub

```
export default class Application {

  navigate(url, push=true) {

  }

  start() {

  }

}
```

This is the form against which we will be coding in this section. We will begin by implementing the `start` method. The first thing we need to do is add an event listener for the `PopStateEvent` (Example 8-5).

Example 8-5. Application class navigate and start methods

```
navigate(url, push=true) {
 console.log(url);
}

start() {
  // create event listener popstate
  this.popStateListener = window.addEventListener('popstate', (e) => {
    let { pathname, search} = window.location;
    let url = `${pathname}${search}`;
    this.navigate(url, false);
  });
}
```

For the time being this event handler simply logs the current URL so that we can confirm that it is working as expected. In "Routing on the Client" on page 77 we will hook in our client-side routing, which will execute a route handler that matches the URL.

Next we need to implement an opt-in click event handler that will be used to execute a route handler when a user clicks on an href or another element that opts-in and provides the required data. The opt in should be declarative and unobtrusive, so that the application framework can easily listen for clicks without impacting the rest of the application. A good mechanism for achieving this goal is using data-* attributes (*http://bit.ly/dataglobalattr*). We can use this interface to define our own data-* attribute and use it to detect click events that should be handled by the application framework (Example 8-6).

Example 8-6. Application class start method event listeners

```
start() {
  // create event listener popstate
  this.popStateListener = window.addEventListener('popstate', (e) => {
    // body omitted for brevity
  });

  // create click listener that delegates to navigate method
  // if it meets the criteria for executing
  this.clickListener = document.addEventListener('click', (e) => {
    let { target } = e;
    let identifier = target.dataset.navigate;
    let href = target.getAttribute('href');

    if (identifier !== undefined) {
      // if user clicked on an href then prevent
      // the default browser action (loading a new HTML doc)
      if (href) {
        e.preventDefault();
      }

      // navigate using the identifier if one was defined.
      // or the href
      this.navigate(identifier || href);
    }
  });
}
```

This implementation places a single event listener on the document, filters by the data attribute data-navigate, and calls a new (yet to be implemented) method called navigate if it meets the identifying criteria. Next, we need to implement the navigate method referenced in the click event handler (Example 8-7).

Example 8-7. Application class navigate and history.pushState methods

```
navigate(url, push=true) {
  // if browser does not support the History API
  // then set location and return
  if (!history.pushState) {
    window.location = url;
    return;
  }

  console.log(url);

  // only push history stack if push
  // argument is true
  if (push) {
    history.pushState({}, null, url);
  }
}
```

The `navigate` method is another placeholder executing a route handler that matches a URL against a path in a routing table. For now we are just pushing an empty state object and a URL onto the history stack to confirm that it works.

Now that we have our stub implementations, we need to update our template for the /{name*} route with some links to test our stubs. Currently the template is a hardcoded string in the `HelloController` class (defined in *./src/hello-controller.js*), because it was simple and did not warrant the overhead of a filesystem read. However, since we are expanding the template, now seems like a good time to move it to a separate file, *./src/hello.html* (Example 8-8).

Example 8-8. Template for HelloController class

```
<p>hello {{fname}} {{lname}}</p>
<ul>
  <li><a href="/mortimer/smith" data-navigate>Mortimer Smith</a></li>
  <li><a href="/bird/person" data-navigate>Bird Person</a></li>
  <li><a href="/revolio/clockberg" data-navigate>Revolio Clockberg</a></li>
</ul>
```

Lastly, we need to update the `HelloController` class (Example 7-7) to read the template from the filesystem, as shown in Example 8-9.

Example 8-9. HelloController class toString method

```
toString(callback) {

  nunjucks.render('hello.html', getName(this.context), (err, html) => {
    if (err) {
      return callback(err, null);
```

```
    }

    callback(null, html);
  });
}
```

If you execute gulp in the terminal and open your browser to *http://localhost:8000*, you should see the new page with the links. You should be able to click through the links, see the address bar update in the browser, and see the log statements in the console. You should see the same behavior when using the browser's forward and backward history controls. We now have our hooks into the browser history!

On the surface these stubs that make use of the History API appear trivial, but they will be the resource request interface to our application, just like the HTTP GET request is on the server. The common factor between the server and client implementations is the URL. It is like the signature of a function. This signature is then used to match a route in a routing table. On the server the routing table is part of hapi. On the client we cannot run hapi, but we should use the same router, so that routes are matched and applied using the same algorithm. In the next section we will explore how this can be accomplished.

Routing on the Client

As you clicked through links and navigated backward and forward through browser history in the previous section, you may have noticed that the hello message on the page did not update as the path parameters changed. This is because we were not executing a controller action and rendering the response. In order to do this we need a client router that uses the same route-matching algorithm as hapi. Fortunately, hapi modularized its HTTP router, call (*https://www.npmjs.com/package/call*), and since Browserify was designed to run Node modules on the client we can use it! But first we need to install it:

```
$ npm install call --save
```

Next we need to import the call module into our application framework client source, *./src/lib/index.client.js*, and code the client implementations for constructor and registerRoutes, as seen in Example 8-10.

Example 8-10. Using the call HTTP router in the Application class

```
import Call from 'call';

export default class Application {

  constructor(routes, options) {
    // save routes as lookup table for controllers
```

```
    this.routes = routes;
    this.options = options;
    // create a call router instance
    this.router = new Call.Router();
    this.registerRoutes(routes);
  }

  registerRoutes(routes) {
    // loop through routes and add them
    // to the call router instance
    for (let path in routes) {
      this.router.add({
        path: path,
        method: 'get'
      });
    }
  }

  navigate(url, push=true) {
    // omitted for brevity
  }

  start() {
    // omitted for brevity
  }

}
```

In the `constructor` and `registerRoutes` methods we used `call` to create our router and register our application routes. These route definitions will be used by the `navigate` method to match URLs to controllers in the `this.routes` property we set in the constructor (Example 8-11).

Example 8-11. Matching routes in the Application class navigate method

```
navigate(url, push=true) {
  // if browser does not support the History API
  // then set location and return
  if (!history.pushState) {
    window.location = url;
    return;
  }

  // split the path and search string
  let urlParts = url.split('?');
  // destructure URL parts array
  let [path, search] = urlParts;
  // see if URL path matches route in router
  let match = this.router.route('get', path);
  // destructure the route path and params
  let { route, params } = match;
```

```
// look up Controller class in routes table
let Controller = this.routes[route];
// if a route was matched and Controller class
// was in the routes table then create a
// controller instance
if (route && Controller) {
  console.log(match)
  console.log(Controller);
}

console.log(url);

// only push history stack if push
// argument is true
if (push) {
  history.pushState({}, null, url);
}
}
```

Executing the Controller Response Flow

Now that we can match URLs to controllers, we can execute the same response flow as we did on the server:

1. Create a controller instance.

2. Execute a controller action.

3. Render a response.

Creating a controller instance

When a controller instance is created, it is passed a context object that contains the path and query parameters. On the server these values are extracted from the request object, which we do not have on the client. In the next chapter we will cover creating lightweight façades for the request and reply objects that will contain abstractions for query and path parameters, but for now we will add the code to the Application class's navigate method:

```
navigate(url, push=true) {
  // preceding code omitted for brevity

  if (route && Controller) {
    const controller = new Controller({
      query: search,
      params: params
    });
  }
```

```
   // following code omitted for brevity
}
```

We now have the ability to create controller instances on the client just as we do on the server. However, you might have spotted an issue in the code. If not, then take another look at how we are populating the `query` property of the `context` object. The value is a string, not an object with decoded values, so we need to parse the `search` value we deconstructed from `urlParts` into an object. If you are like me you have probably written this code numerous times throughout the years, but never filed it off anywhere. Fortunately, others are more organized than me, so we can get a module for just this purpose from npm:

```
$ npm install query-string --save
```

We can import this module and use it to parse the `search` value:

```
navigate(url, push=true) {
  // preceding code omitted for brevity

  if (route && Controller) {
    const controller = new Controller({
      // parse search string into object
      query: query.parse(search),
      params: params
    });
  }
}
```

Now our client application route response implementation passes the expected arguments when creating a controller, so at this point the controller cannot tell if it was constructed on the client or the server. Eureka! We have created our first façade! Again, it's important to keep abstractions to a minimum, and in this case, we're making them in our application framework only because the code is unlikely to change frequently, unlike our application code.

Executing a controller action

Executing the controller action for the instance we created is essentially the same as on the server, as you can see in Example 8-12. The only difference is that we will be passing function stubs for the `request` and `reply` arguments—we will create these façades in the next chapter.

Example 8-12. Executing the controller action in the Application class's navigate method

```
navigate(url, push=true) {
  // preceding code omitted for brevity

  if (route && Controller) {
    const controller = new Controller({
```

```
      // parse search string into object
      query: query.parse(search),
      params: params
    });

    // request and reply stubs; facades will be
    // implemented in the next chapter
    const request = () => {};
    const reply = () => {};
    // execute controller action
    controller.index(this, request, reply, (err) => {
      if (err) {
        return reply(err);
      }
    });
  }
}
```

Rendering a controller response

On the client we need to allow for an alternate rendering implementation for
toString in *./src/lib/Controller.js*:

```
render(target, callback) {
  this.toString(function (err, body) {
    if (err) {
      return callback(err, null);
    }

    document.querySelector(target).innerHTML = body;
    callback(null, body);
  });
}
```

This will allow us to take advantage of different rendering patterns optimized for the
client, such as the React.js virtual DOM (*http://bit.ly/thevirtualdom*), as opposed to a
template library that uses string concatenation.

If you run the default Gulp task in the terminal, open your browser to *http://localhost:
8000/*, and navigate through the links you will now see the page change, but not in the
manner anticipated. The hello message is always "hello hello.html Sanchez". This is
because we have not configured Nunjucks for the client or added a handler on the
server to process template file requests, so each request returns *./src/index.html* and
the controller uses the path parameter "index.html" for fname. Let's fix this. In *.src/
index.client.js* (Example 8-13), we'll configure Nunjucks to read from the absolute
path of */templates* on the browser.

Example 8-13. Configuring Nunjucks for the client

```
import Application from './lib';
import HelloController from './hello-controller';
import nunjucks from 'nunjucks';

// configure nunjucks to read from the dist directory
nunjucks.configure('/templates');

const application = new Application({
  '/hello/{name*}': HelloController
}, {
  // query selector for the element in which
  // the controller response should be injected
  target: 'body'
});

application.start();
```

Now Nunjucks will make Ajax requests for /templates/{*template_file_name*}. Next we need to add a handler to the server to reply with the appropriate template in *./src/index.js*, as seen in Example 8-14.

Example 8-14. Defining a route handler for template files

```
import Hapi from 'hapi';
import Application from './lib';
import HelloController from './hello-controller';
import nunjucks from 'nunjucks';
import path from 'path';

// section omitted for brevity

server.route({
  method: 'GET',
  path: '/templates/{template*}',
  handler: {
    file: (request) => {
      return path.join('dist', request.params.template);
    }
  }
});

// following code omitted for brevity
```

Now if we go back to the browser and navigate through the links we should see the name changing accordingly as we render the controller response as described in Figure 8-1. Success! We now have the basis for our isomorphic JavaScript application! However, we left behind a bit of mess, so in the next section we will do some house-keeping.

We are making a non-cached Ajax call for every template in this example. This isn't very efficient, but it is simple, defers loading, and works well when developing. In some cases you will want to precompile your templates for the client, and sometimes the server as well.

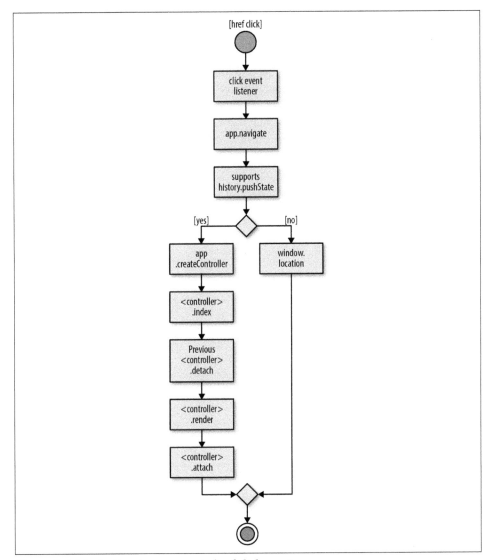

Figure 8-1. Navigation in response to href click event

Organizing Our Code

We've accomplished our goal of transporting our framework and application code to the client. It works well, but we duplicated some code in our application, in *./src/index.js* and *./src/index.client.js*. For instance, our application instantiation and initialization code, which contains the route definitions, appears in both files. This duplication of route definitions is not ideal because when we add, remove, or modify a route we have to remember to do it in two different places. Additionally, we have muddled our application code with environment implementation details. As the application grows over time these files will likely become out of sync and more difficult to maintain. We can improve the maintainability by moving the environment details to options files, so that *./src/index.js* is easier to read and becomes the entry point for both the client and the server. Let's start by creating the server options file, *./src/options.js*, and moving the environment-specific details to this new file (Example 8-15).

Example 8-15. Application options for the server

```
import Hapi from 'hapi';
import path from 'path';
import nunjucks from 'nunjucks';

const server = new Hapi.Server({
  debug: {
    request: ['error']
  }
});
server.connection({
  host: 'localhost',
  port: 8000
});

const APP_FILE_PATH = '/application.js';
server.route({
  method: 'GET',
  path: APP_FILE_PATH,
  handler: (request, reply) => {
    reply.file('dist/build/application.js');
  }
});

server.route({
  method: 'GET',
  path: '/templates/{template*}',
  handler: {
    file: (request) => {
      return path.join('dist', request.params.template);
    }
```

```
  }
});

export default {
  nunjucks: './dist',
  server: server,
  document: function (application, controller, request, reply, body, callback) {
    nunjucks.render('./index.html', {
      body: body,
      application: APP_FILE_PATH
    }, (err, html) => {
      if (err) {
        return callback(err, null);
      }
      callback(null, html);
    });
  }
};
```

We then need to do the same for the client by creating *./src/options.client.js* (Example 8-16).

Example 8-16. Application options for the client

```
export default {
  target: 'body',
  nunjucks: '/templates'
};
```

Now we need to update our the property in our *package.json* file to reflect these changes:

```
{
  "browser": {
    "./src/lib/index.js": "./src/lib/index.client.js",
    "./src/options.js": "./src/options.client.js"
  }
}
```

Finally, we need to update *./src/index.js* to use the new configuration modules, as shown in Example 8-17.

Example 8-17. Unified application entry point

```
import Application from './lib';
import HelloController from './HelloController';
import nunjucks from 'nunjucks';
import options from './options';

nunjucks.configure(options.nunjucks);
```

```
const application = new Application({
  '/hello/{name*}': HelloController
}, options);

application.start();
```

These small changes should help ease development and maintenance costs immensely as the application grows over time.

Summary

In this chapter we took our framework and application code from the server to the client, making it an isomorphic code base. We familiarized ourselves with common build patterns and leveraged the History API to respond to URL changes in the browser using the same lifecycle as we did on the server. We will continue to build upon this work in the next chapter, where we will create lightweight façades to some commonly needed features of isomorphic applications.

Completed Code Examples

You can install the completed code examples from this chapter by executing `npm install thaumoctopus-mimicus@"0.4.x"` in your terminal.

CHAPTER 9

Creating Common Abstractions

Jason Strimpel

In this chapter we will create two abstractions that are frequently needed by isomorphic JavaScript applications:

1. Getting and setting cookies
2. Redirecting requests

These abstractions provide a consistent API across the client and server by encapsulating environment-specific implementation details. Throughout Part II there have been numerous warnings about the dangers of abstraction, (including Coplien's *abstraction is evil*). Given these warnings, and the fact that this entire chapter is about creating abstractions, let's take a moment to discuss when and why to abstract.

When and Why to Use Abstraction

Abstraction is not really evil, but rather frequently misused, prematurely obfuscating important details that provide context to code. These misguided abstractions are usually rooted in a valiant effort to make people's lives better. For example, a module that sets up project scaffolding is useful, but not if it hides details in submodules that cannot be easily inspected, extended, configured, or modified. It is this misuse that is often perceived as evil, and all abstraction is then labeled evil by association. However, if properly applied, abstraction is an invaluable design tool for helping to create an intuitive interface.

In my experience, I have used abstraction to normalize APIs across environments in cases where the environmental differences would have burdened the users with implementation details beyond what they should be concerned with for the layer in which they are working. Or, as Captain Kirk would say, I abstract when "the needs of the many outweigh the needs of the few" (or "the one"). That guiding principle may work well for running a starship, but that alone doesn't make the decision to abstract correct. It is very difficult to know when to abstract. Typically I ask myself a few questions, such as:

- Do I have enough domain knowledge and experience with the code to even make the decision?
- Am I making too many assumptions?
- Is there a more suitable tool than abstraction?
- Will the benefits provided by abstraction outweigh the obfuscation costs?
- Am I providing the right level of abstraction at the correct layer?
- Would abstraction hide the intrinsic nature of the underlying object or function?

If your answers to these questions and similar ones indicate that abstraction is a good solution, then you are probably safe to proceed. However, I would still encourage you to discuss your ideas with a colleague. I cannot count the number of times where I have overlooked a crucial piece of information or alternative that makes abstraction not the best solution for a problem.

Now that we have cleared up the when and why of abstraction as much as possible, let's proceed with creating some abstractions.

Getting and Setting Cookies

Cookies are plain-text values that were originally created to determine if two server requests had come from the same browser. Since then, they have served many purposes, including as a client-side data store. Cookies are sent as header values by the browser and the server. Both the browser and the server have the ability to get and set cookie values. As such, the ability to read and write cookies uniformly in an isomorphic JavaScript application is a common necessity, and this is a prime candidate for abstraction. The case for abstraction when reading and writing cookies is that the interface can differ greatly between the client and the server. Additionally, at the application level, intimate knowledge of the environment implementation details does not provide any value as one is either simply reading or writing a cookie. Creating a façade that abstracts these details does not obfuscate useful information from the application developer any more than the URL abstracts useful information—the inner workings of the Web—from a user.

Defining the API

A cookie is comprised of key/value pairs separated by equals signs, with optional attributes that are delimited by semicolons:

```
HTTP/1.0 200 OK
Content-type: text/html
Set-Cookie: bnwq=You can't consume much if you sit still and read books;
Expires=Mon, 20 Apr 2015 16:20:00 GMT
```

The HTTP cookie in this example is sent as part of the request header to the server or received in the response header by the browser. This uniform exchange format allows the client and server to implement interfaces for getting and setting these values. Unfortunately, the interfaces are not consistent across environments. This is because on servers, unlike in browsers, there is not a standard interface. This is by design because server responsibilities are varied and they differ greatly from browsers, which are intended to be platforms for running (W3C) standards-based user interfaces. These differences are precisely why we are creating an abstraction. However, before we can create a common interface for getting and setting cookies across the client and the server we need to know the different environment interfaces—i.e., we need to gain the domain knowledge required to create a proper abstraction.

Getting and setting cookies on the client

`document.cookie` (*http://bit.ly/documentcookie*) is the browser interface for getting and setting cookies. `console.log(document.cookie)` will log all cookies that are accessible by the current URL. The key/value pairs returned by `document.cookie` are delimited by semicolons:

```
Story=With Folded Hands;Novel=The Humanoids
```

This string of values isn't of much use, but it can easily be transformed in an object with the cookie names as the keys, or we can implement a function to retrieve a cookie value by name as seen here:

```
function getCookieByName(name) {
  let cookies = document.cookie.split(';')

  for (let i = 0; i < cookies.length; i++) {
    let [key, value] = cookies[i].split('=');
    if (key === name) {
      return value;
    }
  }
}
```

The interface for setting a cookie is the same, except the righthand side of docu ment.cookie is assigned a cookie value:

```
document.cookie="bnwq=A love of nature keeps no factories busy;path=/"
```

Getting and setting cookies on the server

As noted in "Defining the API" on page 88, server implementations for getting and setting cookies can differ. In Node cookies can be retrieved from the response header using the http module, as shown in Example 9-1.

Example 9-1. Getting cookie by name on a Node server

```
import http from 'http';

function getCookieByName(name, cookies) {
  for (let i = 0; i < cookies.length; i++) {
    let [key, value] = cookies[i].split('=');
    if (key === name) {
      return value;
    }
  }
}

http.createServer(function (request, response) {
  let someCookie = getCookieByName('some-cookie', request.headers.cookies);
  response.end('Hello World\n');
}).listen(8080);
```

Throughout the book we have been using hapi as our application server. Hapi has a more convenient interface, as illustrated in Example 9-2.

Example 9-2. Getting cookie by name on the server using hapi

```
import Hapi from 'hapi';

const server = new Hapi.Server({
  debug: {
    request: ['error']
  }

  server.route({
    method: 'GET',
    path: {anything*},
    handler: (request, reply) => {
      let someCookie = request.state['some-cookie'];
      reply('Hello World\n');
    }
  });
});

server.start();
```

Setting a cookie in Node using the http module is fairly straightforward (Example 9-3).

Example 9-3. Setting a cookie on a Node server

```
import http from 'http';

http.createServer(function (request, response) {
    response.writeHead(200, {
        'Set-Cookie': 'some-cookie=some value',
        'Content-Type': 'text/plain'
    });
    response.end('Hello World\n');
}).listen(8080);
```

Setting a cookie using hapi is equally easy (Example 9-4).

Example 9-4. Setting cookie on the server using hapi

```
import Hapi from 'hapi';

const server = new Hapi.Server({
    debug: {
        request: ['error']
    }

    server.route({
        method: 'GET',
        path: {anything*},
        handler: (request, reply) => {
            reply('Hello World\n').state('some-cookie', 'some value');
        }
    });
});

server.start();
```

Creating an interface

Now that we have a better understanding of how cookies work on both the client and the server, we are ready to create a standard interface for getting and setting cookies. The interface (Example 9-5) will be the contract against which we code the environment-specific implementations.

Example 9-5. Isomorphic cookie interface

```
class Cookie {

    // name (String): cookie name
    // value (String): cookie value
    // options.secure (Boolean): https only
    // options.expires (Number): expiration time in milliseconds
    // options.path (String): restrict cookie to a specific path
```

```
// options.domain (String): restrict cookie to a specific domain
// Returns: Undefined
set(name, value, options = {}) {

}

// name (String): cookie name
// Returns: cookie value (String); default null
get(name) {

}

}
```

The interface described in Example 9-5 needs to be accessible in route handler controller instances, so that application developers can make use of the API during the request/response lifecycle and after the controller is bound on the client. A good candidate that meets these requirements is the context object that is created when the controller is constructed:

```
constructor(context) {
    this.context = context;
}
```

Implementing the interface for the client

Now that we have defined the interface, we can code the client implementation. In "Getting and setting cookies on the client" on page 89, we saw some cookies were simple implementations to help illustrate the basics of working with the native browser API. In reality, getting and setting cookies requires a bit more work, such as encoding values properly.

Encoding Cookies

Technically cookies do not have to be encoded, other than semicolons, commas, and whitespace. But most implementations that you will see, especially on the client, URL-encode the values and names. The more important part is to encode and decode the values consistently across the client and the server, and to be careful not to double-encode values. These concerns are addressed in Example 9-6 and Example 9-7.

Fortunately, there are numerous libraries available that unobtrusively handle these details. In our application we will be using cookies-js (*https://www.npmjs.com/package/cookies-js*), which we can install as follows:

```
$ npm install cookies-js --save
```

Now we can use `cookies-js` to code against the interface defined in Example 9-5. The client cookie implementation (*./lib/cookie.client.js*) is shown in Example 9-6.

Example 9-6. Client cookie implementation, ./lib/cookie.client.js

```
import cookie from 'cookies-js';

export default {

  get(name) {
    return cookie.get(name) || undefined;
  },

  set(name, value, options = {}) {
    // convert milliseconds to seconds for cookies-js api
    if (options.expires) {
      options.expires / 1000;
    }
    cookie.set(name, value, options);
  }

}
```

Implementing the interface for the server

The server implementation (*./lib/cookie.js*), shown in Example 9-7, will simply wrap the hapi `state` interface.

Example 9-7. Server cookie implementation

```
export default function (request, reply) {

  // encoding functions http://www.rfc-editor.org/rfc/rfc6265.txt
  // follows same patterns as 'cookies-js' that is used on the client
  function cleanName(name) {
    name = name.replace(/[^#$&+\^`|]/g, encodeURIComponent);
    return name.replace(/\(/g, '%28').replace(/\)/g, '%29');
  }

  function cleanValue(value) {
    return (value + '').replace(/[^!#$&-+\--:<-\[\]-~]/g, encodeURIComponent);
  }

  return {

    get(name) {
      return request.state[name] && decodeURIComponent(request.state[name]) ||
        undefined;
    },
```

```
    set(name, value, options = {}) {
      reply.state(cleanName(name), cleanValue(value), {
        // use hapi defaults if values are falsy
        isSecure: options.secure || false,
        path: options.path || null,
        ttl: options.expires || null,
        domain: options.domain || null
      });
    }

  };

}
```

Including the cookie implementations

Now that we have our implementations defined, we need to include them in the request lifecycle (Examples 9-8 and 9-9).

Example 9-8. Including the client cookie implementation in ./lib/index.client.js

```
// code omitted for brevity
import cookie from './cookie.client';
// code omitted for brevity

export default class Application {
  // code omitted for brevity
  navigate(url, push=true) {
    // code omitted for brevity
    const controller = new Controller({
      // parse search string into object
      query: query.parse(search),
      params: params,
      cookie: cookie
    });
    // code omitted for brevity
  }
  // code omitted for brevity
}
```

Example 9-9. Including the server cookie implementation in ./lib/index.js

```
import cookieFactory from './cookie';

export default class Application {
  // code omitted for brevity
  addRoute(path, Controller) {
    // code omitted for brevity
    const controller = new Controller({
      query: request.query,
      params: request.params,
```

```
      cookie: cookieFactory(request, reply)
    });
    // code omitted for brevity
  }
}
```

Cookie example

Now we should be able to set and get cookies on both the client and the server, as shown in Example 9-10.

Example 9-10. Isomorphic set cookie example in HelloController class (Example 7-7) index method, ./src/HelloController.js

```
index(application, request, reply, callback) {
  this.context.cookie.set('random', '_' + (Math.floor(Math.random() * 1000) + 1),
  { path: '/' });
  callback(null);
}
```

Figure 9-1 shows how our isomorphic cookie getter and setter works.

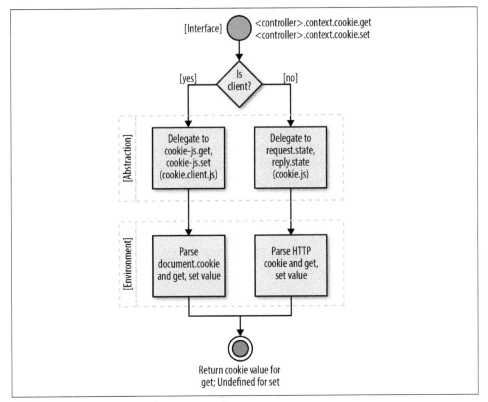

Figure 9-1. Isomorphic cookie getter and setter

Redirecting a Request

Another common need across the client and the server is the ability to redirect user requests. Redirects allow a single resource to be accessible by different URLs. Some use cases for redirects are vanity URLs, application restructuring, authentication, managing user flows (e.g., checkout), etc. Historically only the server has handled redirects, by replying to the client with an HTTP redirect response:

```
HTTP/1.1 301 Moved Permanently
Location: http://theoatmeal.com/
Content-Type: text/html
Content-Length: 174
```

The client uses the location specified in the redirect response to make a new request, ensuring the user receives the actual resource he initially requested.

Another important piece of information in the redirect response is the HTTP status code. The status code is used by search engines, another type of client, to determine if a resource has been temporarily or permanently relocated. If it has been permanently relocated (status code 301), then all the ranking information associated with the previous page is transferred to the new location. Because of this, it is vital that redirects are handled correctly on the server.

Defining the API

In "Getting and Setting Cookies" on page 88, we learned that there is not a consistent way to set cookies on the server, but that there is a standard contract for sending the information over the Internet. The same is true of redirects on the server. The client does not have the concept of creating HTTP redirects, but it does have the ability to update the location (URL), which makes a new HTTP request. As with getting and setting cookies, the API is consistent across browsers. Again let's follow best practices and better familiarize ourselves with the environments for which we will be creating an abstraction before we define an interface.

Redirecting on the client

`window.location` (*http://bit.ly/windowlocation*) is the API for redirection on the client. There are a couple of different ways to update the location, as shown in Example 9-11.

Example 9-11. Redirecting on the client

```
window.location = 'http://theoatmeal.com/';
// OR
window.location.assign('http://theoatmeal.com/');
```

Redirecting on the server

In Node, the http module can be used to facilitate redirects (see Example 9-12).

Example 9-12. Redirecting on a Node server

```
import http from 'http';

http.createServer(function (request, response) {
   response.writeHead(302, {
     'Location': 'http://theoatmeal.com/',
     'Content-Type': 'text/plain'
   });
   response.end('Hello World\n');
}).listen(8080);
```

In hapi redirects can be a bit less verbose (Example 9-13).

Example 9-13. Redirecting on the server using hapi

```
import Hapi from 'hapi';

const server = new Hapi.Server({
  debug: {
    request: ['error']
  }

  server.route({
    method: 'GET',
    path: {anything*},
    handler: (request, reply) => {
      reply.redirect('http://theoatmeal.com/');
    }
  });
});

server.start();
```

Creating an interface

Redirection should be available during the request/response lifecycle, so that an application can redirect requests when necessary. In our case this is when the controller's action method, index, is being executed. On the server we already have direct access to hapi's redirect interface, reply.redirect. However, on the client we have a no-operation reply function, const reply = () => {};, so we need to add redirect functionality to this function. We have two options:

1. Create a façade for the hapi `reply` object for the server and do the same for the client.

2. Add a redirect API with the same signature as hapi to the client `reply` stub.

If we go with option 1 we have the freedom to create an API of our choosing, but then we have to design the interface and create two implementations. Additionally, is it a good idea to wrap the entire hapi `reply` object just so we can define our own redirect interface? This isn't a very good reason to create an abstraction of that magnitude. If we go with option 2 then we have to adhere to the hapi redirect interface, but we have less code to maintain and fewer abstractions. The less we abstract the better, especially early on, so let's go with option 2.

Implementing the interface for the client

We will be using the hapi redirect interface as the guide for our client implementation. We will only be implementing the `redirect` (*http://hapijs.com/api/#response-object-redirect-methods*) function, as seen in Example 9-14. The other methods will be no-operations since they are used to set HTTP status codes, which are irrelevant on the client. However, we will still need to add these methods so that if one of the methods is called on the client it will not throw an error.

Example 9-14. Redirecting on the client implementation (./src/lib/reply.js)

```
export default function (application) {

  const reply = function () {};

  reply.redirect = function (url) {
    application.navigate(url);
    return this;
  };

  reply.temporary = function () {
    return this;
  },

  reply.rewritable = function () {
    return this;
  },

  reply.permanent = function () {
    return this;
  }

  return reply;

}
```

Including the client implementation

Now that we have defined the implementation, we need to include it in the request lifecycle. We can do this by adding the code in Example 9-15 to *./lib/index.client.js*.

Example 9-15. Including the client redirect implementation in ./lib/index.client.js

```
// code omitted for brevity
import replyFactory from './reply.client';
// code omitted for brevity

export default class Application {
  // code omitted for brevity
  navigate(url, push=true) {
    // code omitted for brevity
    const request = () => {};
    const reply = replyFactory(this);
    // code omitted for brevity
  }
  // code omitted for brevity
}
```

Redirection example

In the examples thus far the entry point for the HelloController has been /hello/{name*}. This works great, but what if we want the users to see the greeting message when they access the application root, *http://localhost:8000/*? We could set up another route that points to this controller, but what if we only wanted to show this message the first time a user access the application? Our cookie and redirect APIs can handle this (see Example 9-16).

Example 9-16. HomeController class redirection example (./src/HomeController.js)

```
import Controller from './lib/Controller';

export default class HomeController extends Controller {

  index(application, request, reply, callback) {
    if (!this.context.cookie.get('greeting')) {
      this.context.cookie.set('greeting', '1', {
        expires: 1000 * 60 * 60 * 24 * 365 });
    }

    return reply.redirect('/hello');
  }

  toString(callback) {
    callback(null, 'I am the home page.');
  }
```

```
}
```

Next we need to add our new controller to a route:

```
const application = new Application({
  '/hello/{name*}': HelloController,
  '/': HomeController
}, options);
```

Finally, let's add a new link to *hello.html*, so that we can navigate to/on the client:

```
<p>hello  </p>
<ul>
  <li><a href="/hello/mortimer/smith" data-navigate>Mortimer Smith</a></li>
  <li><a href="/hello/bird/person" data-navigate>Bird Person</a></li>
  <li><a href="/hello/revolio/clockberg" data-navigate>Revolio Clockberg</a></li>
  <li><a href="/" data-navigate>Home Redirect</a></li>
</ul>
```

Now when we access *http://localhost:8000/* on the client or the server it will redirect us to *http://localhost:8000/hello*. This approach provides us with the flexibility to implement different conditional redirects and to set the HTTP codes accordingly.

Figure 9-2 illustrates our isomorphic redirect abstraction.

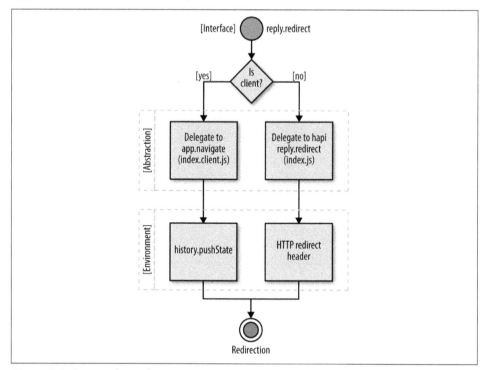

Figure 9-2. Isomorphic redirect

Summary

In this chapter we created a couple of common abstractions—getting and setting cookies, and redirects—that are needed by most isomorphic JavaScript applications. We also learned when and why to use abstraction within the context of building isomorphic JavaScript apps. These examples and this knowledge will help us make more informed decisions in the future when we are deciding whether or not to use abstraction, and to use it properly if we have a case that calls for it.

Completed Code Examples

You can install the completed code examples from this chapter by executing `npm install thaumoctopus-mimicus@"0.5.x"` in your terminal.

CHAPTER 10

Serializing, Deserializing, and Attaching

Jason Strimpel

In Chapter 8 we added the ability to execute the request/reply lifecycle on the client. In Chapter 9 we created isomorphic abstractions for getting and setting cookies and redirecting user requests. These additions took our application framework from a server-only solution to a client-and-server solution. These were great strides toward a more complete solution, but we are still missing a key component of an isomorphic JavaScript application: the ability to seamlessly pick up on the client where things left off on the server.

Essentially, the application should take the server-rendered markup and bind itself to the markup just as if it had been rendered on the client like an SPA. This means that any data used to render the controller response on the server should be available on the client, so that when a user starts interacting with an application she is able manipulate the data, e.g., via a form. Any DOM event handlers will need to be bound as well, to facilitate user interaction. In order to "rehydrate" on the client, four steps must be completed:

1. Serialize the data on the server.
2. Create an instance of the route handler controller on the client.
3. Deserialize the data on the client.
4. Attach any DOM event handlers on the client.

Defining Rehydration

You will see the term "rehydration" used throughout the rest of this chapter and in other isomorphic JavaScript references. Rehydration in the context of isomorphic JavaScript applications is the act of regenerating the state that was used to render the page response on the server. This could include instantiating controller and view objects, and creating an object or objects (e.g., models or POJOs (*https://en.wikipedia.org/wiki/Plain_Old_Java_Object*)) from the JSON that represents the data used to render the page. It could also include instantiating other objects, depending on your application architecture.

The remainder of this chapter will focus on implementing these processes in our application.

Serializing Data

So far in the examples in this book, we have used cookies, path and query parameters, and hardcoded defaults. In the real world, applications also rely on data from remote sources such as REST (*https://en.wikipedia.org/wiki/Representational_state_transfer*) or GraphQL (*http://bit.ly/graphqlintro*) services. In JavaScript apps, this data is ultimately stored in a POJO, or plain old JavaScript object. The data is used in conjunction with HTML and DOM event handlers to create user interfaces. On the server only the HTML portion of the interface is created because the DOM bindings cannot be done until the server response has been received and processed by the client. The processing, rehydration, and DOM binding on the client often relies on this state data from the server. Additionally, user interactions that trigger events after the rehydration and binding typically need access to this data to modify it or make decisions. Therefore, it's important that the data be accessible by the client during rehydration and afterward. Unfortunately, the POJO cannot be sent across the network as part of an HTTP request. The POJO needs to be serialized to a string that can be passed to the template, parsed by the client, and assigned to a global variable.

The serialization is accomplished using `JSON.stringify` (*http://bit.ly/jsonstringify*), which creates a string representation of the POJO. This is the standard method for serializing a POJO, but we still need to add a method to our `Controller` class from Example 7-3 that can be executed on the server and that returns this stringified POJO:

```
serialize() {
  return JSON.stringify(this.context.data || {});
}
```

For our application the default implementation is serializing the `this.context.data` property from *./src/lib/controller.js*. However, this default behavior could be easily overridden to handle different use cases. Sometimes there are APIs for setting and getting data in a POJO, such as Backbone models (*http://backbonejs.org/#Model*) or Redux (*http://redux.js.org/*) stores (`store.getState`). For these and other client data stores the `serialize` function can be easily overridden to implement custom behavior for serializing these objects.

 The data that is being serialized by the `Controller` class's `serial ize` method will typically be sourced from a remote location, as noted earlier. This data is usually resolved using HTTP as the transport mechanism. This is done on the client using Ajax and on the server using Node's `http` module. This data fetching requires client-specific implementations. Fortunately, we are not the first developers to need an isomorphic HTTP client. There are many, but a few popular ones are isomorphic-fetch (*https://www.npmjs.com/package/isomorphic-fetch*) and superagent (*https://www.npmjs.com/package/superagent*).

Next we need to update the `document` function from Example 8-15 (*./src/options.js*) to call the new `serialize` function, as seen in Example 10-1.

Example 10-1. Server options call to Controller class serialize method

```
export default {
  nunjucks: './dist',
  server: server,
  document: function (application, controller, request, reply, body, callback) {
    nunjucks.render('./index.html', {
      body: body,
      application: APP_FILE_PATH,
      state: controller.serialize(),
    }, (err, html) => {
      if (err) {
        return callback(err, null);
      }
      callback(null, html);
    });
  }
};
```

Finally, we create a global variable in our template (*./src/index.html*) that can be accessed during rehydration on the client:

```
<script type="text/javascript">
  window.__STATE__ = '{{state}}';
</script>
```

Make sure to add this <script> tag before the <script> tag that includes the application source.

Creating a Controller Instance

The next step in the rehydration process is to create a controller instance on the client for the current route. This instance will be assigned the serialized data and bound to the DOM, which will enable the user to interact with the HTML interface returned by the server. Fortunately, we have already written the code to look up a Controller class using the router and create a controller instance. We just need to reorganize the code a bit so that we can reuse it.

In the navigate function we created in Example 8-4 we used the URL to look up the Controller class in the application route table. If one was found, we then created a controller instance. This code can be moved to a new function in the Application class (*./src/lib/index.client.js*) that can be called by the navigate function, defined in Example 10-2.

Example 10-2. Client Application class createController method

```
createController(url) {
  // split the path and search string
  let urlParts = url.split('?');
  // destructure URL parts array
  let [path, search] = urlParts;
  // see if URL path matches route in router
  let match = this.router.route('get', path);
  // destructure the route path and params
  let { route, params } = match;
  // look up Controller class in routes table
  let Controller = this.routes[route];

  return Controller ?
    new Controller({
      // parse search string into object
      query: query.parse(search),
      params: params,
      cookie: cookie
    }) : undefined;
}
```

Now we can use the createController function in the navigate function and a function that we are about to create, rehydrate (Example 10-3).

Example 10-3. Client Application class navigate method updates and rehydrate method

```
// encapsulates code that is used in the rehydrate method and
// the popStateListener in the start method
getUrl() {
  let { pathname, search} = window.location;
  return `${pathname}${search}`;
}

rehydrate() {
  this.controller = this.createController(this.getUrl());
}

navigate(url, push=true) {
  // if browser does not support the History API
  // then set location and return
  if (!history.pushState) {
    window.location = url;
    return;
  }

  let previousController = this.controller;
  this.controller = this.createController(url)

  // REMAINDER OF FUNCTION BODY OMITTED FOR BREVITY
  // see the complete example in the "Attaching DOM Event
  // Handlers" section of this chapter
}
```

The rehydrate function can then be called by the start function (Example 10-4).

Example 10-4. Client Application class start method

```
start() {
  // PREVIOUS CODE OMITTED FOR BREVITY
  // the rehydrate call has been added to the bottom
  // of the function body
  this.rehydrate();
}
```

Idempotence and Rehydration

In our application examples controller construction is simple. However, in some cases the construction or initialization logic could be more complex. In those cases it is important that the component initialization logic be *idempotent*. This is a fancy way of saying that no matter how many times a function is executed, the result should be the same. If you are relying on closures, counters, and so on in your initialization and the initialization logic is not idempotent, then the rehydration process could produce errors. For example, if there is an application singleton that has state, any component initialization logic that relies on that state will differ on the client if the state is not transferred to the client and added to the singleton on the client before rehydration begins.

Deserializing Data

In the previous section we created an instance of the controller during the application rehydrate process on the client. Now we need to transfer the state that was created on the server and serialized as part of the server page response to the controller instance on the client. This is necessary because routes can have different states, and the application will depend upon these states. For instance, if the route rendered on the server has any sort of interface for interacting with or manipulating data, such as an "add to cart" button, a form, a graph with a range selector, etc., then the user will likely need that data to interact with the page, rerender the page, or persist a change.

In "Serializing Data" on page 104 we included the state data in the page response, so now all we have to do is implement a `deserialize` method on the base controller (*./src/lib/controller.js*):

```
deserialize() {
  this.context.data = JSON.parse(window.__STATE__);
}
```

Global Variables

Relying on a global variable is typically bad practice because of potential name collisions and maintenance issues. However, there isn't a real alternative. You could pass the data into a function, but then you would expose a function as a global in some fashion.

This method can now be used as part of the rehydration process to assign the data to the controller instance. We can add data rehydration to the client `Application` class's `rehydrate` method (in *./src/lib/index.client.js*) as follows:

```
rehydrate() {
  this.controller = this.createController(this.getUrl());
```

```
    this.controller.deserialize();
  }
```

Attaching DOM Event Handlers

The last part of the rehydration process is attaching event handlers to the DOM. In its simplest form, event binding is done by calling the native method, addEventLis tener, as shown here:

```
document.querySelector('body').addEventListener('click', function (e) {
  console.log(e);
}, false);
```

Some libraries set the context for the event listener functions to the view or controller object that created the listener. Some libraries, like Backbone (*http://backbonejs.org/#View-events*), have an interface for defining event listeners. These event listeners are bound to the containing view element using event delegation (*https://learn.jquery.com/events/event-delegation/*) to reduce overhead in the browser. In our case we are just going to add an empty method, attach, to the controller that is called during the rehydration process. It will be up to the application developer to implement the method details:

```
attach(el) {
  // to be implemented by the application
}
```

In addition to the rehydration process, the attach method should be called as part of the client-side route response lifecycle. This ensures that a route handler will be bound to the DOM regardless of whether it was executed on the client or the server. Example 10-5 shows how we add DOM binding to the client Application class's rehy drate method.

Example 10-5. Adding DOM binding to the rehydrate method

```
rehydrate() {
  let targetEl = document.querySelector(this.options.target);

  this.controller = this.createController(this.getUrl());
  this.controller.deserialize();
  this.controller.attach(targetEl);
}
```

These two calls to the attach method ensure that a route handler is always bound to the DOM. However, there is a bit of an issue with this code—there is not a yin for our yang. If we continually attach handlers to the DOM without detaching a previous handler, we could end up with a memory leak (*http://www.html5rocks.com/en/tutori als/memory/effectivemanagement/*). Adding a detach method to the base controller and calling it as part of the client-side route handler lifecycle, as shown in Example 10-6, can help prevent this problem. detach will be an empty method like attach, leaving the implementation details up to the application developer:

```
detach(el) {
  // to be implemented by the application
}
```

Example 10-6. Complete navigate method for client Application class

```
navigate(url, push=true) {
  // if browser does not support the History API
  // then set location and return
  if (!history.pushState) {
    window.location = url;
    return;
  }

  let previousController = this.controller;
  this.controller = this.createController(url)

  // if a controller was created then proceed with navigating
  if (this.controller) {
    // request and reply stubs
    const request = () => {};
    const reply = replyFactory(this);

    if (push) {
      history.pushState({}, null, url);
    }

    // execute controller action
    this.controller.index(this, request, reply, (err) => {
      if (err) {
        return reply(err);
      }

      let targetEl = document.querySelector(this.options.target);
      if (previousController) {
        previousController.detach(targetEl);
      }
      // render controller response
      this.controller.render(this.options.target, (err, response) => {
        if (err) {
          return reply(err);
        }

        reply(response);
        this.controller.attach(targetEl);
      });
    });
  });
```

```
    }
}
```

Verifying the Rehydration Process

Now that we have the core pieces in place that enable an application to recall state and attach itself to the DOM, we should be able to rehydrate our app. To test recalling state, first let's generate a random number in the `index` method of the `HelloControl ler` class (Example 7-7) and store it as a property in `this.context.data`:

```
index(application, request, reply, callback) {
  this.context.cookie.set('random', '_' + (Math.floor(Math.random() * 1000) + 1),
    { path: '/' });
  this.context.data = { random: Math.floor(Math.random() * 1000) + 1 };
  callback(null);
}
```

Next, we need to add `this.context.data` to the rendering context for the `toString` method in `HelloController`:

```
toString(callback) {
  // this can be handled more eloquently using Object.assign
  // but we are not including the polyfill dependency
  // for the sake of simplicity
  let context = getName(this.context);
  context.data = this.context.data;

  nunjucks.render('hello.html', context, (err, html) => {
    if (err) {
      return callback(err, null);
    }

    callback(null, html);
  });
}
```

We can now render this random number in the *hello.html* template:

```
<p>hello {{fname}} {{lname}}</p>
<p>Random Number in Context: {{data.random}}</p>
<ul>
  <li><a href="/hello/mortimer/smith" data-navigate>Mortimer Smith</a></li>
  <li><a href="/hello/bird/person" data-navigate>Bird Person</a></li>
  <li><a href="/hello/revolio/clockberg" data-navigate>Revolio Clockberg</a></li>
  <li><a href="/" data-navigate>Home Redirect</a></li>
</ul>
```

Next, we can log `this.context.data` in our `attach` method and compare the values:

```
attach(el) {
  console.log(this.context.data.random);
}
```

We can also add a click listener in our `attach` method to verify that the correct target is being passed to this method and that an event listener can be bound to it:

```
attach(el) {
  console.log(this.context.data.random);
  el.addEventListener('click', function (e) {
    console.log(e.currentTarget);
  }, false);
}
```

Next, we need to ensure that we clean up the event handler we added in our `attach` method. If we don't do this, then we will have an event handler for each navigation to the `/hello/{name*}` route. First we need to move the event listener function from the `attach` method to a named function, so that we can pass a reference to the function when we remove it. At the top of the `HelloController` class, let's create a function expression:

```
function onClick(e) {
  console.log(e.currentTarget);
}
```

Now we can update our `attach` method and add a `detach` method:

```
attach(el) {
  console.log(this.context.data.random);
  this.clickHandler = el.addEventListener('click', onClick, false);
}

detach(el) {
  el.removeEventListener('click', onClick, false);
}
```

If you reload the page and click anywhere, you should see the body element in the console. If you navigate, clear the console, and click again, you should only see one log statement because our `detach` method removed the event listener from the previous route.

Figure 10-1 shows a high-level overview of what we're aiming for.

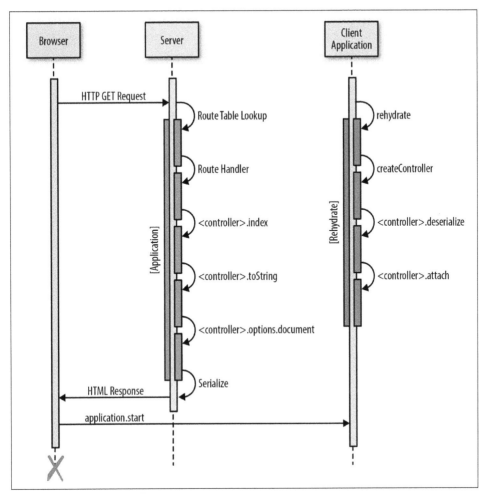

Figure 10-1. Client rehydration

Summary

We learned a lot in this chapter. Here's a quick recap of what we walked through:

- Serializing the route data in the server page response
- Creating an instance of the route handler on the client
- Deserializing the data
- Attaching the route handler to the DOM

These rehydration steps ensure that an application functions the same for a user regardless of whether the route was rendered on the client or the server, with the added performance benefit of not refetching the data.

Completed Code Examples

You can install the completed code examples from this chapter by executing `npm install thaumoctopus-mimicus@"0.6.x"` in your terminal.

CHAPTER 11

Closing Thoughts

Jason Strimpel

We covered a lot of material in Part II, which provided a solid understanding of how isomorphic JavaScript applications work. Armed with this knowledge you can now evaluate and amend existing solutions, or create something entirely new to meet your specific needs. However, before you venture out into this brave new world, a bit of reflection on what we have covered will help you to be even better equipped to take the next steps into isomorphic development. We will begin this process with a quick review of what we built in Part II, why we built it, and its limitations.

Production Readiness

Throughout Part II we progressively built an application core and a simple example that leveraged the core. While this was instrumental in learning the concepts, we don't recommend using this core in a production application. The core was written solely for this book as a learning device. There are better production-ready libraries for handling common functionality like managing session history, such as `history` (*https://www.npmjs.com/package/history*). `history` and other modules were intentionally not utilized in order to focus on learning the underlying concepts and native APIs as opposed to learning a library API. However, leveraging highly adopted and well-supported open source solutions is a good idea because these libraries will likely cover edge cases that we might not have accounted for in our code.

Knowing How Much Structure Is Needed

In Part II we emphasized creating a common request/response lifecycle, which is something that you may or may not need. For instance, if you are going to buy wholesale into a technology such as React (*https://facebook.github.io/react/*), then you might not need this level of abstraction. There are many articles on the Web, like

"Exploring Isomorphic JavaScript" (*http://nicolashery.com/exploring-isomorphic-javascript/*) that illustrate how simple it is to create an isomorphic solution using React and other open source libraries.

Just remember the trade-off—the Web and related technologies are going to change, and complete application rewrites are rarely approved by companies (and when they are approved, they frequently fail). If you want to adapt to change, then a very thin layer of structure will allow you to easily test out new technologies and migrate legacy code in phases. Of course, you need to balance abstraction with the expected life of the application, use case details, and other factors.

Change Is a Constant

Rapid change in the Web is not only evident from history, but in the current mindset of the community that you should always use a transpiler. We are now writing code as if change is imminent—because it is. A new version of JavaScript will be released annually now. And keep in mind that this new release schedule only represents a fraction of the change you will face. Patterns, libraries, and tools are evolving even more rapidly. So be prepared!

Managing Change

Come gather 'round people
Wherever you roam
And admit that the waters
Around you have grown
And accept it that soon
You'll be drenched to the bone
If your time to you
Is worth savin'
Then you better start swimmin'
Or you'll sink like a stone…

    —Bob Dylan, *The Times Are a Changin'*

While this song was intended to describe an entirely different concept, a good portion of the lyrics aptly describe the daily, weekly, monthly, and yearly struggles a web developer faces: responding to change. There is a constant wave of excitement over the latest browser APIs, newest libraries, language enhancements, and emerging development and application architecture patterns—so much so that it can feel like your worth as a developer and the quality of your applications are sinking in the midst of all the rising change.

Fortunately, even with this ever-increasing rate of change, isomorphic JavaScript applications will remain consistent (at least in terms of their lifecycle), so you have a constant in a sea of variables. This is because their design is based on the Web's HTTP request/reply lifecycle. A user makes a request for a resource using a URL and the server responds with a payload. The only difference is that this lifecycle is used on both the client and the server, so there are a few key points in the lifecycle that you need to be cognizant of when making architectural and implementation decisions:

Routing
> There should be a router that can map a URL to a function.

Execution
> The function should execute in an asynchronous fashion—i.e., there should be a callback that is executed once processing is complete.

Response/rendering
> Once execution is complete, rendering should occur in an asynchronous manner.

Serializing
> Any data retrieved and used during the execution and rendering phases should be part of the server response.

Deserializing
> Any objects and data need to be recreated on the client, so that they are available on the client during runtime when a user is interacting with the application.

Attaching
> The event handlers should be bound, so that the application is interactive.

It is that simple. All the rest of the hype is just enhancements and implementation details. How you stitch these steps together and the libraries you utilize to do so is entirely up to you. For instance, you could choose to loosely glue together open source solutions, or you could create a more formalized lifecycle like we did in this part of the book, into which you can plug the latest JavaScript libraries.

Keep the Application Core Small

Just remember that the more patterns and standards you add to your reusable application core, the less flexible it becomes, which makes it more susceptible to breakage over time when adapting to change. For instance, a team that I worked on decided to standardize on Backbone and RequireJS when we created an isomorphic JavaScript framework because these libraries were popular at the time. Since then, new patterns and libraries have emerged. These standards have made it difficult to adapt to change at the application level. The trick is finding the balance that offers value while still being flexible.

The degree to which you add structure to support a formalized lifecycle should be contingent upon your concern for the need to respond to change. This need to respond to change should also be balanced with the expected life of the application. If it is going to be replaced in a few years, then it might not be worth the overhead of a formalized lifecycle. The need for standardization—i.e., whether you will be building more than a single application—should also be considered.

If you want the ability to fully respond to change at any time, then creating an application core that allows inversion of control (*https://en.wikipedia.org/wiki/Inversion_of_control*) for swapping out libraries should be of high importance to you. Lastly, don't let anyone tell you what you need or don't need. You know your use case, your colleagues' needs, the business's needs, and the customers' needs better than anyone.

Conclusion

That's it for Part II. We hope you enjoyed the journey as much as we did. However, we are not done yet. We saved the best for last. Industry experts have graciously donated their time to share their real-world experiences in Part III. I encourage you to read on and absorb every ounce of wisdom they have to share. I did, and as a result I have a much more enriched view of the landscape and the Web to come.

PART III

Real-World Solutions

It's been a great year for isomorphic JavaScript. Since we started writing this book, we've seen the isomorphic JavaScript landscape change and evolve. The JavaScript language and server-side JavaScript environments are maturing and are gaining more adoption. JavaScript is becoming a dominant language with an incredible ecosystem of libraries that run on both the browser and the server.

Developers from different backgrounds are converging on JavaScript. At the O'Reilly Fluent Conference (*http://conferences.oreilly.com/fluent/javascript-html-us*) this year we had the opportunity to meet many developers who are starting to use the concepts and implementations we've discussed in this book. We also had a chance to sit down with some of the thought leaders of the JavaScript community. During our discussions we discovered that, in a lot of cases, the real wedge for Node.js into the enterprise space is in fact isomorphic JavaScript. Isomorphic JavaScript is the real game changer that forces many teams—in some cases teams that are very used to a different server stack—to reluctantly acknowledge the benefits of JavaScript on the server. It is becoming harder to deny the significance of isomorphic JavaScript especially with its implications for initial page load performance and search engine indexing and optimization.

So far, this book has focused on providing the foundational knowledge required to build an isomorphic JavaScript application. We've introduced the concepts around isomorphic JavaScript apps and built a seed project that implements these concepts. In this part of the book, we will explore existing solutions in the market today, looking at various frameworks that have adopted (or will soon adopt) isomorphic Java-Script. We'll also see examples of isomorphic projects at different companies in different situations using different technology stacks. These case studies outline the many kinds of problems teams have to solve when building isomorphic JavaScript apps. We hope this part provides a third dimension to the overall picture, illustrating approaches you might consider when adopting isomorphic JavaScript.

CHAPTER 12

Isomorphic React.js at WalmartLabs

Jason Strimpel and Maxime Najim

We are going through an application architecture metamorphosis at WalmartLabs (*http://www.walmartlabs.com/*). We are just now slowly beginning to emerge from our warm, secure Java cocoon and have started to spread our beautiful isomorphic JavaScript wings. It is this transition that we will be sharing in this chapter.

Origin of a Species

Walmart has undergone many changes since early 2013. This is because executive leadership set the wheels in motion years ago to make the digital and physical experience seamless for Walmart customers. A large part of this has been an investment in technology and infrastructure. It has been an evolutionary process. Some technologies and projects have thrived and others have become extinct. So it goes. Extinctions have occurred for a variety of reasons, but we learn from each and move forward. One of the latest and most germane to this book is the gradual extinction of Java and Backbone + Handlebars in the UI layer in Walmart.com (*http://walmart.com*). In the world of software nothing really dies unless the business or a particular initiative dies. The same problem is just solved in a different (and hopefully better) way using other technologies (Figure 12-1).

Figure 12-1. In the world of software, nothing really dies

The problems we faced with Walmart.com are now being addressed with React.js and Node.js.

The Problem

Typically people see the problem to be solved as simply achieving feature parity with an existing solution—i.e., delivering Walmart.com. While achieving feature parity using a newly developed, unproven technology stack is not a trivial undertaking, that in itself does not provide any real value to the business or the customer. It just moves the eggs from one basket to another.

The real problem is not just delivering Walmart.com, but rather considering how it is delivered and how that delivery solution scales across multiple tenants and clients. Even this problem definition fails to adequately describe the true scope of the problem and the potential for value add by a new technology stack. The real value is determined by whether the new technology and processes can achieve the following guiding principles better than the previous solution:

- Attract and retain engineering talent
- Increase development velocity
- Improve code quality

Ultimately these guiding principles translate to reducing engineering costs to the business and delivering better experiences to the customer, faster. For instance, switching to a single language and runtime container that can be deployed across servers and clients increases development velocity, which in turn allows the business to quickly deliver product enhancements and services across channels. This also reduces development costs. Another example is providing engineers with tools and technologies that they are passionate about using. This will help to attract and retain talent. It will help improve the stack and developer knowledge, because a community will organically arise around these technologies. Lastly, if you select a technology that is flexible but still defines a rendering lifecycle, event interface, and composition pattern, then code quality will improve because there will be clear standards for these core UI patterns. If not, engineers across the organization will make the same decisions multiple times with different design outcomes, which causes reusability and integration issues and increases development costs.

There are too many examples to enumerate, but if you focus your solution and decisions on the guiding principles outlined here, then you will be much better off than if you just ride the latest technology bandwagon for the sake of popularity.

The Solution

As noted earlier, at Walmart the problem is being solved by React and Node. This is because these technologies met our needs and aligned with our goals of attracting and retaining talent, increasing development velocity, and improving code quality—in addition to solving the typical issues addressed by any isomorphic JavaScript solution by providing all of the following:

- SEO support
- Distributed rendering
- Single code base
- Optimized page load
- Single stack/rendering lifecycle

React also allowed us to easily share encapsulated pieces of UI rendering logic (i.e., components) across tracks, which greatly improved reusability and the quality of the components as numerous tracks enhanced them. It also provided a common interface for application developers to construct web and native mobile UIs. Furthermore, it provided a great composition model and the community had already defined composition patterns/best practices, such as container components, and presentation components that we could follow. Additionally, the low cost of rerendering the entire UI afforded by the virtual DOM makes UI state management much simpler than the approach of programmatically cherry-picking and manipulating sections of the DOM in application code. Finally, the React community is very active and there are numerous supporting libraries, patterns, and case studies for building and maintaining applications.

React Boilerplate and Patterns

Before we cover the specific approach Walmart took, we will outline the common boilerplate and patterns for an isomorphic React application.

Assumptions and Further Information

The following code examples assume basic knowledge of React (*https://facebook.github.io/react/*), JSX (*https://facebook.github.io/react/docs/jsx-in-depth.html*), and ES6 (*http://es6-features.org/*). If you are looking to get started with React or create an isomorphic React application, there are numerous examples and boilerplate projects available online to help you get started.

Rendering on the Server

The general approach is to run a Node web framework such as hapi (*http://hapijs.com/*) or Express (*http://expressjs.com/*) and call React's `renderToString` method. There are many variations to this, but its simplest form can be seen in Example 12-1.

Example 12-1. Render component to string

```
import Hapi from 'hapi';
import React from 'react';
import { renderToString } from 'react-dom/server';
import html from './html';
import Hello from './hello';

class Hello extends React.Component {
 render() {
  return <div>Hello {this.props.text}!</div>;
 }
}

const server = new Hapi.Server({
  debug: {
    request: ['error']
  }
});
server.connection({
  host: 'localhost',
  port: 8000
});

server.route({
  method: 'GET',
  path:'/{42*}',
```

```
    handler: (request, reply) => {
      reply(html({
        html: renderToString(<Hello text="World"/>)
      }));
    }
});

server.start((err) => {
  if (err) {
    throw err;
  }

  console.log('Server running at:', server.info.uri);
});
```

The HTML string from the Hello component is rendered to the template that is returned as the handler response, as seen in Example 12-2.

Example 12-2. HTML document template

```
export default function (context) {
  return (`
    <html lang="en">
      <head>
        <meta charSet="utf-8" />
      </head>
      <body>
        <div id="content">${context.html}</div>
        <!--
          this would be a webpack or browserify bundle
          <script src="${context.js}"></script>
          -->
      </body>
    </html>
  `);
}
```

This approach works well for static sites in which components do not rely on data on the client. To ensure that this data makes it to the client, a step is added to serialize any data used when rendering on the server (Example 12-3).

Example 12-3. Serialize data (handler from Example 12-1)

```
server.route({
  method: 'GET',
  path:'/{42*}',
  handler: (request, reply) => {
    // this could be data from a service, DB, etc.
    const data = { text: 'World' };
    reply(html({
```

```
        data: `window.__DATA__ = ${JSON.stringify(data)};`,
        html: renderToString(<Hello text={data.text} />)
    }));
  }
});
```

This data is then passed to the template along with the HTML string, as seen in
Example 12-4.

Example 12-4. HTML document template with data

```
export default function (context) {
  return (`
    <html lang="en">
      <head>
        <meta charSet="utf-8" />
        <script>${context.data}</script>
      </head>
      <body>
        <div id="content">${context.html}</div>
        <!--
          this would be a webpack or browserify bundle
          <script src="${context.js}"></script>
        -->
      </body>
    </html>
  `);
}
```

The next enhancement usually added is a router that can be shared across the server
and the client. This is necessary because without a way to match URLs to handlers—
components, in this case—every URL would return the same response. The most
commonly used router is the `react-router` (*https://github.com/reactjs/react-router*)
because it was designed to work with React and is a React component itself. The typical approach is to use the `react-router` `match` function to map incoming requests to
a route, as shown in Example 12-5.

Example 12-5. Matching routes on the server

```
import Hapi from 'hapi';
import React from 'react';
import { renderToString } from 'react-dom/server';
import { match, RouterContext, Route } from 'react-router';
import html from './html';

// code omitted for brevity...

const wrapper = (Component, props) => {
  return () => {
```

```
    return <Component {...props} />
  }
}

server.route({
  method: 'GET',
  path:'/{42*}',
  handler: (request, reply) => {
    // this could be data from a service, DB, etc.
    const data = { text: 'World' };
    const location = request.url.path;
    const routes = (
      <Route path="/" component={wrapper(Hello, data)} />
    );

    match({routes, location}, (error, redirect, props) => {
      if (error) {
        // render 500 page
        return;
      }

      if (redirect) {
        return reply.redirect(`${redirect.pathname}${redirect.search}`);
      } else if (props) {
        return reply(html({
          data: `window.__DATA__ = ${JSON.stringify(data)};`,
          html: renderToString(<RouterContext {...props} />)
        }));
      }
    });

    // render 404 page
    return;
  }
});
```

Quite a bit of new code was introduced in this example. Let's break it down:

- wrapper is used to inject props into react-router route handlers.

- The react-router match function is used in conjunction with the path (loca
  tion) to determine if there is a matching route.

- If props exists, then a route was matched and the RouterContext—i.e., the route
  handler component, which is the wrapped Hello component in this case—is rendered.

Modularizing the Code

In the real world this code would be split into reusable modules that can be shared across the client and the server. To keep things simple, the code is kept in a single block/module here.

Resuming on the Client

The previous section described the fundamental steps that most isomorphic React applications execute when rendering on the server. Everyone has their own slightly different implementation, but in the end an HTML document consisting of markup from the rendering of the React component tree to a string and related data is sent to the client. It is then up to the client to pick up where the server left off. In isomorphic React applications this is done simply by calling `React.render` on the DOM node where the output from `renderToString` was injected on the server (see Example 12-6).

Example 12-6. Rendering on the client

```
import React from 'react';
import ReactDOM from 'react-dom';

class Hello extends React.Component {
  render() {
    return <div>Hello {this.props.text}!</div>;
  }
}

const props = window.__DATA__;

ReactDOM.render(<Hello {...props} />, document.getElementById('content'));
```

Rendering on the Client and Server

The `return` value of component `render` methods should not differ between the client and the server, given the same data. If they do, then the DOM will be rerendered when `ReactDOM.render` is called, which can cause performance issues and degrade the user experience. To prevent this, make sure the data passed to components is the same on the client and the server for a given route.

Example 12-6 will rerender the component tree, applying any differences between the virtual DOM created by `ReactDOM.render` and the actual DOM. It will also bind all component event listeners (among other things; see the React documentation (*https://facebook.github.io/react/docs/component-specs.html*)). The same principle applies when using the `react-router`, as illustrated in Example 12-7.

Example 12-7. Rendering on the client with the react-router

```
import React from 'react';
import ReactDOM from 'react-dom';
import { Router, browserHistory } from 'react-router'

class Hello extends React.Component {
 render() {
  return <div>Hello {this.props.text}!</div>;
 }
}

const wrapper = (Component, props) => {
  return () => {
    return <Component {...props} />
  }
}
const props = window.__DATA__;
const routes = (
  <Route path="/" component={wrapper(Hello, props)} />
);

ReactDOM.render(<Router history={browserHistory} routes={routes} />,
  document.getElementById('content'));
```

This approach works really well because now routes can be shared between the client and the server. The last piece of the puzzle is ensuring that any rehydrated data is passed to the components. This is usually handled by a wrapper or provider component that resolves data for the component tree (e.g., `react-resolver` (*https://github.com/ericclemmons/react-resolver*), `async-props` (*https://github.com/ryanflorence/async-props*), Redux (*http://redux.js.org/*), etc.). However, we are using the `wrapper` approach just as we did on the server for simplicity.

Virtual DOM and Checksums

React uses a virtual DOM (*https://facebook.github.io/react/docs/glossary.html*) to represent a component rendering tree when `render` is called. This virtual DOM is compared with the DOM and any differences are patched. So, when `ReactDOM.render` is called on the client, there shouldn't be any differences and only the event listeners will be bound. The mechanism that React uses to do this is `data-react-checksum` attributes, which are covered in "Component Rendering Optimization" on page 131.

That is all it takes to get a simple isomorphic React application up and running. As you can see, these steps are easily translated to the steps described in Part II, with some being combined and occurring implicitly (e.g., `ReactDOM.render` binds event listeners and creates component instances).

The Walmart Approach

Walmart uses a variant of the approach described in "React Boilerplate and Patterns" on page 124. The primary difference is that we do not transition to an SPA after the first page load. The reasoning is that this is an optimization. It is not required for a minimal viable product (MVP), a complete migration of Walmart.com, nor is it part of our primary objectives (described in "The Problem" on page 122). However, we still serialize and rehydrate on the client. At a high level, these are the steps that occur when a route is matched on the server:

- An application that responds to a subset of routes is initialized.
- The application creates a redux (*http://redux.js.org/*) store and bootstrap actions are fired that prime the store with data in response to a request.
- The react-router (*https://github.com/reactjs/react-router*) matches a particular route.
- The matched route is then rendered using the react-dom/server renderTo String method using the redux store and other data.
- The response is sent to the client including serialized redux store data.

Then, on the client:

- The client initializes the redux store with data serialized from the server.
- The react-dom render method is called on the application (a React provider/wrapper component) and the react-router.

Easy, right? Maybe to describe at a high level. There were actually many challenges. One of these will be highlighted in the next section.

Overcoming Challenges

> The first cut is always sh*t.
>
> —Jason Strimpel

No matter how talented you are or how much you prepare, something will always go wrong. Mistakes will be made or unknowns will arise and wreak havoc on your best-designed and carefully executed plan. How you react to these challenges is what counts. Many challenges were encountered and are still being encountered with Walmart's migration from Java and Backbone + Handlebars to React and Node. This is the story of one of these challenges.

Time to First Byte

When we started migrating to React, we immediately found that our Time to First Byte (TTFB) was not on par with our existing apps. Server-side CPU profiling revealed that a majority of the time was being spent in ReactDOMServer's renderTo String code to render the initial markup on the server.

 Time to First Byte is a standard way of measuring the responsiveness of a web application server. As the name indicates, this is simply the time it takes for the browser to receive the first byte of the page. A slow TTFB is an indication that the application server is taking a long time to process the request and generate the response.

It turns out that React's server-side rendering can become a performance bottleneck for pages requiring many virtual DOM nodes. On large pages, ReactDOMServer.ren derToString(..) can monopolize the CPU, block Node's event loop, and starve out incoming requests to the server. That's because for every page request, the entire page needs to be rendered—even fine-grained components, which, given the same props, always return the same markup. CPU time is wasted in unnecessarily rerendering the same components for every page request. We knew that in order for React to work for us we had to change something fundamental to the framework in order to reduce the rendering time on the server.

Component Rendering Optimization

We decided to trade space for CPU time. We applied two complimentary optimizations: *component memoization* and *component templatization.*

Component memoization

We had an intuition. We knew that given the same props, pure components will always return the same HTML markup. Similar to a pure function in functional programing, a pure component is simply a function of props, which means it should be possible to *memoize* (or cache) the rendered results to speed up rendering significantly after the first response. So the question became: could we optimize the React rendering time on our servers by avoiding the need to rerender the same components with the exact same props?

After peeling through the React code base we discovered React's mountComponent function. This is where the HTML markup is generated for a component. We knew that if we could intercept React's instantiateReactComponent module by using a require hook we could avoid the need to fork React and inject our memoization optimization. Example 12-8 a simplified version of the injected cache optimization we implemented.

Example 12-8. Caching a component on the server using a require hook

```
const InstantiateReactComponent = require("react/lib/instantiateReactComponent");

...

const WrappedInstantiateReactComponent = _.wrap(InstantiateReactComponent,
  function (instantiate) {
    const component = instantiate.apply(
      instantiate, [].slice.call(arguments, 1));
    component._instantiateReactComponent = WrappedInstantiateReactComponent;
    component.mountComponent = _.wrap(
      component.mountComponent,
      function (mount) {
        const cacheKey = config.components[cmpName].keyFn(
          component._currentElement.props);
        const rootID = arguments[1];
        const cachedObj = lruCache.get(cacheKey);
        if (cachedObj) {
          return cachedObj.markup.replace(
            new RegExp('data-reactid="' + cachedObj.rootId, "g"),'data-reactid="' +
              rootID);
        }
        const markup = mount.apply(
          component, [].slice.call(arguments, 1));
        lruCache.set(cacheKey, {
          markup: markup,
          rootId: rootID
        });

    return markup;
    });
  }
  return component;
});

Module.prototype.require = function (path) {
  const m = require_.apply(this, arguments);
  if (path === "./instantiateReactComponent") {
    return WrappedInstantiateReactComponent;
  }
  return m;
};
```

As you can see, we keep a Least Recently Used (LRU) cache that stores the markup of rendered components (replacing the data-reactid attribute appropriately). We also wanted the ability to memoize any pure component, not just those that implement a certain interface, so we created a configurable component caching library that accepts a map of component names to a cacheKey generator function. It looks something like Example 12-9.

Example 12-9. Configurable component caching library

```
var componentCache = require("@walmart/react-component-cache");

var cacheKeyGenerator = function (props) {
   return props.id + ":" + props.name;
};

var componentCacheRef = componentCache({
  components: {
    'Component1': cacheKeyGenerator,
    'Component2': cacheKeyGenerator
  },
  lruCacheSettings: {
  // LRU cache options, see below
  }
});
```

Application owners can opt into this caching by specifying the component's name and referencing the cacheKey generator function. This function returns a string representing all inputs into the component's rendering and is used as a cache key for the rendering optimization. Subsequent renderings of the component with the same name will have a cache hit and return the cached result.

Our goal for using React in the first place was to reuse components across different pages and apps, so we already had a set of reusable pure components with well-defined interfaces. These pure components always return the same result given the same props, and they don't depend on the state of the application. Because of that, we were able to use the configurable component caching code shown here and memoize most of the components in our page's global header and footer without having to make any code changes to the components themselves.

Component templatization

This solution took us far in our goal to reduce the CPU footprint on our servers. But we wanted to take this caching optimization a step further and enable component templatization to allow cached rendered markup to include more dynamic data. Even though pure components "should" always render the same markup structure, there are certain props that might be more dynamic than others. Take for example the simplified React product component in Example 12-10.

Example 12-10. React product component

```
var React = require('react');

var ProductView = React.createClass({
  render: function() {
    var disabled = this.props.inventory > 0 ? '' : 'disabled';
```

```
      return (
        <div className="product">
          <img src={this.props.product.image}/>
          <div className="product-detail">
            <p className="name">{this.props.product.name}</p>
            <p className="description">{this.props.product.description}</p>
            <p className="price">Price: ${this.props.selected.price}</p>
            <button type="button" onClick={this.addToCart} disabled={disabled}>
              {this.props.inventory ? 'Add To Cart' : 'Sold Out'}
            </button>
          </div>
        </div>
      );
  }
});

module.exports = ProductView;
```

This component takes props like product image, name, description, and price. If we were to apply the component memoization described previously, we'd need a cache large enough to hold all the products. Moreover, less frequently accessed products would likely have more cache misses. This is why we added the component templatization feature. This feature requires classifying properties in two different groups:

Template attributes
  Set of properties that can be templatized. For example, in a `<link>` component, the `url` and `label` are template attributes since the structure of the markup does not change with different `url` and `label` values.

Cache key attributes
  Set of properties that impact the rendered markup. For example, the `availabilityStatus` of an item impacts the resulting markup (e.g., generating an "Add To Cart" button versus a "Get In-Stock Alert" button, along with pricing display, etc.).

These attributes are configured in the component caching library, but instead of providing a `cacheKey` generator function you'd pass in the `templateAttrs` and `keyAttrs` instead (see Example 12-11).

Example 12-11. Configurable component caching library with template and key attributes

```
"use strict";
// Example component cache that can be used templatized
var componentCache = require("@walmart/react-component-cache");

var componentCacheRef = componentCache({
    components: {
      "ProductView": {
```

```
        templateAttrs: ["product.image", "product.name", "product.description",
          "product.price"],
        keyAttrs: ["product.inventory"]
      },
      "ProductCallToAction": {
        templateAttrs: ["url"],
        keyAttrs: ["availabilityStatus", "isAValidOffer", "maxQuantity",
          "preorder", "preorderInfo.streetDateType", "puresoi",
          "variantTypes", "variantUnselectedExp"
        ]
      }
    }
  }
});
```

Notice that the template attributes for `ProductView` are all the dynamic props that would be different for each product. In this example, we also used the `product.inventory` prop as a cache key attribute since the markup changes based on inventory logic to enable the "Add To Cart" button.

When template attributes are configured, the corresponding props are switched with template delimiters (i.e., `${ prop_name }`) during the React component rendering cycle. The template is then compiled, cached, and executed to hand the markup backup to React. The cache key attributes are used to cache the template. For subsequent requests, the component's render is short-circuited with a call to the compiled template. Example 12-12 shows the component caching library with template attributes and template delimiters.

Example 12-12. Component caching library with templatization

```
component.mountComponent = _.wrap(
    component.mountComponent,
    function (mount) {
      const cacheKey = ...
      const rootID = arguments[1];
      // Iterate over configured template attributes
      // and set template delimiters on props
      templateAttrs.forEach((attrKey) => {
        const _attrKey = attrKey.replace(".", "_");
        templateAttrValues[_attrKey] = _.get(curEl.props, attrKey);
        _.set(curEl.props, attrKey, "${" + _attrKey + "}");
      });
      const cachedObj = lruCache.get(cacheKey);
      if (cachedObj) {
        const cacheMarkup = restorePropsAndProcessTemplate(
          cachedObj.compiled,
          templateAttrs,
          templateAttrValues,
        curEl.props);
        return cacheMarkup.replace(
```

```
                new RegExp('data-reactid="' + cachedObj.rootId, "g"),
                    'data-reactid="' + rootID);
    }
    const markup = mount.apply(component, [].slice.call(arguments, 1));
    const compiledMarkup = _.template(markup);
    self.lruCache.set(cacheKey, {
      compiled: compiledMarkup,
      rootId: rootID
    });
    return restorePropsAndProcessTemplate(
      compiledMarkup,
      templateAttrs,
      templateAttrValues,
      curEl.props);
});
```

In the `restorePropsAndProcessTemplate(..)` function we take the template attributes, set the attribute key props, and execute the template with attribute values:

```
const restorePropsAndProcessTemplate = (
  compiled, templateAttrs, templateAttrValues, props
) => {
    templateAttrs.forEach((attrKey) => {
      const _attrKey = attrKey.replace(".", "_");
      _.set(props, attrKey, templateAttrValues[_attrKey]);
    });
    return compiled(templateAttrValues);
};
```

Performance Improvements

By applying the memoization and templatization optimizations we were able to improve the mean request time by 40% and the 95-percentile request time by nearly 50%. These optimizations freed up more of the event loop on our Node servers and allowed them to do what Node does best: asynchronous data fetching. The result was lower CPU time for each page request and more concurrent requests that are not blocked on `renderToString(..)`. As you can see in Figure 12-2, the CPU profiles of one server request after applying the optimizations looked much better.

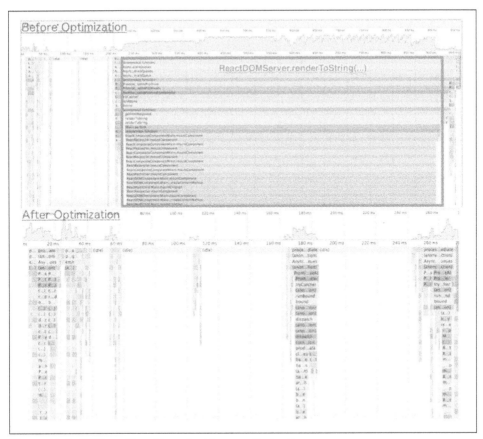

Figure 12-2. CPU profile with and without optimization

If we were to highlight all the cached markup that was returned to a sample page, it would look something like Figure 12-3 (the shaded area indicates markup that was cached on the server).

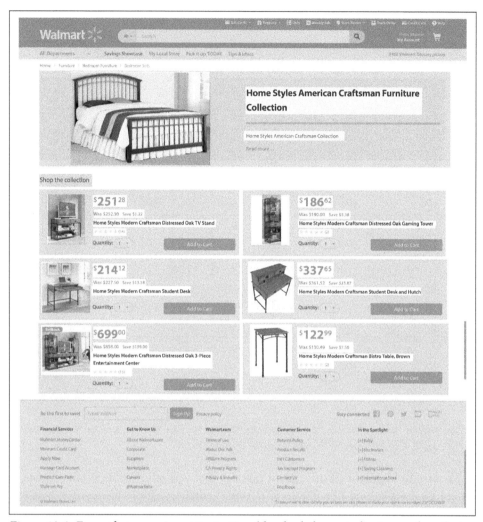

Figure 12-3. Example page using optimization (the shaded area indicates markup that was cached)

It is important to note that there are several other independent projects that are endeavoring to solve the React server-side rendering bottleneck. Projects like `react-dom-stream` (*https://github.com/aickin/react-dom-stream*) and `react-server` (*https://github.com/redfin/react-server*) attempt to deal with the synchronous nature of `React DOM.renderToString` by rendering React pages asynchronously. Streaming React rendering helps on the server by preventing synchronous render processing from starving out other concurrent requests. Streaming the initial HTML markup also means that browsers can start painting the page earlier (without having to wait for the entire response). These approaches help improve the user's perception of performance since content can be painted sooner on the screen. However, the total CPU time remains the same since an equivalent amount of work needs to be done on the server, whether it is done synchronously or asynchronously. In contrast, component memoization and templatization reduce the total amount of CPU time for subsequent requests that rerender the same components again. These rendering optimizations can be used in conjunction with other performance enhancements like asynchronous rendering.

Next Steps

The next steps for us at Walmart will be to continue to identify and fix performance bottlenecks like the problem discussed in "Overcoming Challenges" on page 130. Eventually, when we are ready, we will flip the isomorphic switch and take advantage of the SPA model for subsequent "page" renders. Finally, we will be open sourcing everything!

Acknowledgments

Anyone who has undergone a similar transformation knows it is not easy, especially in a company the size of Walmart. Aside from the technical and scaling challenges, there are organizational, cultural, and resource challenges. Fortunately, there has been great collaboration, vision, and leadership across teams. This whole endeavor has been an organization-wide team effort, but we wanted to thank the leadership at WalmartLabs for making the investment. We also wanted to thank Alex Grigoryan (*https://www.linkedin.com/in/alexgrigoryan*) in particular for supporting the production of this chapter and allowing us to share the story of the transformation he has been leading. Lastly, we wanted to thank Jack Herrington (*https://www.linkedin.com/in/jherr*) for initiating and inspiring this change, and for all the groundbreaking work he drove and delivered. We will never forget your jars of change video.

Postscript

We have come a long way, and we feel privileged to have played a part, if an extremely minor one, in this journey. The best part, at least from our perspective, is that this journey has just begun, which means that there are many opportunities to engineer more great solutions to difficult problems. So if you are looking for a challenge, we strongly encourage you to take a look at the opportunities at WalmartLabs. Lastly, make sure to follow @walmartlabs (*https://twitter.com/WalmartLabs*) on Twitter, watch the GitHub organization (*https://github.com/walmartlabs*), and peruse the WalmartLabs Engineering blog (*https://medium.com/walmartlabs*), as we will be sharing our journey in more detail and our code with the community!

CHAPTER 13

Full Stack Angular

Jeff Whelpley

In December 2012 I joined GetHuman. My first assignment was an interesting one. I needed to figure out a way to build a rich, real-time version of our popular flagship website, GetHuman.com (*https://gethuman.com/*). The challenge was essentially figuring out a way to combine two things that (at that time) did not often go together:

1. A client-side JavaScript web app
2. An SEO-friendly, performance-driven website

I had a wealth of experience with each of these separately, but never together. The most common solutions at that time for meeting these requirements usually boiled down to a Rails-like approach or a headless browser–based approach—both of which had significant downsides.

The Rails approach involved building a server-side website with small bits of JavaScript sprinkled on various pages. While this approach did a really good job for SEO and performance, it did not allow me to take advantage of advanced client-side features. Moreover, this solution felt like a traditional website, which is not what we wanted. We wanted a fast, responsive, and fluid user experience, which you typically could only achieve at that time with a client-driven, single-page application (SPA).

On the other end of the spectrum were the apps built completely on the client side using Backbone, Angular, Ember, or just plain vanilla JS. In order to make sure your client-side app was visible in search engines you would use a headless browser like PhantomJS to cache snapshots of your client-side application views. This sort of worked, but there were two big issues with headless browsers:

1. They are too slow to use at runtime.
2. They are too resource-intensive to use for sites that contain hundreds of thousands of pages, like GetHuman.

Clearly neither of these solutions was going to work for us. So, what could we do?

Isomorphic JavaScript: The Future of Web Apps

After trying out various client/server setups in an attempt to meet our needs, I ran across an article (*http://nerds.airbnb.com/isomorphic-javascript-future-web-apps/*) from Spike Brehm where he described a new approach to web development that he had implemented at Airbnb: isomorphic JavaScript. As Spike put it:

> At the end of the day, we really want a hybrid of the new and old approaches: we want to serve fully-formed HTML from the server for performance and SEO, but we want the speed and flexibility of client-side application logic.

> To this end, we've been experimenting at Airbnb with "Isomorphic JavaScript" apps, which are JavaScript applications that can run both on the client-side and the server-side.

This was exactly what we were looking for! Spike had perfectly described the thing that I couldn't quite put into words; the thing that I had been searching for during the better part of 2013.

There was just one problem.

Conceptually I was completely in sync with Spike, but his specific Backbone-based solution was not exactly what I was looking for. I knew Backbone very well, but I preferred a relatively new framework, Angular.js. So why didn't I just make Angular isomorphic, just like how Spike made Backbone isomorphic?

If you know anything about Angular.js, you know that this is easier said than done.

Isomorphic Angular 1

In order to implement server-side rendering in Backbone, Spike created a completely separate library called Rendr (*https://github.com/rendrjs/rendr*). He didn't modify the existing Backbone library at all. I took a similar approach with Angular. Just like Backbone, Angular is tightly coupled to the DOM. So, the only ways to render on the server would be to either shim all of the client-side DOM objects like the window and browser, or create a higher-level API that your application can code against. We went with the former solution, which required us to build a layer of abstraction above Angular very similar to how Rendr works with Backbone.

After over a year of experimenting, testing, and iterating, we finally arrived at an elegant solution.

Similar to Rendr, we created a library called Jangular (*https://github.com/gethuman/jangular*) that allowed us to render our Angular web application on the server. The new GetHuman.com rendered the server view almost instantly, even under heavy load. After a of couple seconds the Angular client takes over the page and it comes to life with several real-time features. We thought we had solved the server-side rendering puzzle!

Unfortunately, there were a few issues with our Angular 1 server rendering solution:

1. Jangular only supported a subset of Angular. Jangular could easily have been expanded, but we decided to initially only support the pieces of Angular we needed for GetHuman.com.
2. Jangular enforced fairly rigid conventions, like a specific folder hierarchy, file-naming standards, and code structure.

In other words, we created a solution that worked great for us, but was difficult for anyone else to use.

ng-conf 2015

A couple of months after creating Jangular, I was invited to speak at ng-conf about our server rendering solution in Angular 1. Igor Minar, the technical lead for the Angular team at Google, reviewed my "Isomorphic Angular" slides before the conference and mentioned that what I was trying to do would be a lot easier in Angular 2. I didn't quite understand at the time, but he told me that they had created an abstraction layer that should make it easy to render an Angular 2 app on the client or the server or anywhere else. So, I added a brief mention at the end of my ng-conf talk about the potential for server rendering being baked into the Angular 2 core. I said:

> I think it is only a matter of time (whether I do it or I know a lot of other people that are going to be interested in this as well) [to leverage] all this new stuff in Angular 2 and [use] on some of the other stuff I've worked on [to build] a really awesome Isomorphic solution that everybody can use.

Right after my presentation, I met someone named Patrick Stapleton (also known as PatrickJS) who was just as interested as I was in isomorphic JavaScript. Patrick brought up the idea of us working together to make server rendering in Angular 2 a reality.

It didn't take us long. One week after ng-conf, Patrick had some success (see Figure 13-1).

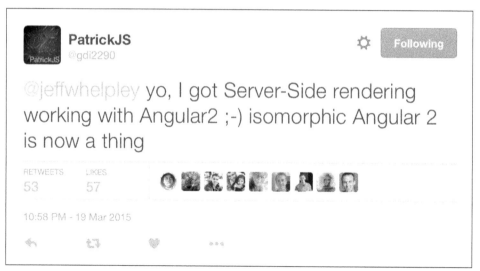

Figure 13-1. Isomorphic Angular 2!

After a flurry of discussions with developers from the Angular community and core team members, Brad Green, head of the Angular team, hooked us up with Tobias Bosch, the mastermind behind the Angular 2 rendering architecture. The three of us got to work.

Angular 2 Server Rendering

Three months later we had a working prototype and a much better understanding of the Angular 2 rendering architecture. In June 2015, we gave a presentation at Angu-larU on our Angular 2 server rendering solution.

You can watch this presentation online via YouTube (*http://whlp.ly/server-rendering*).

The following is a summary of that talk.

Use Cases for Server Rendering

Each of these use cases provides a possible answer to the question: why is server rendering important for your client-side web app?

Perceived load time

The initial load of a client-side web application is typically very slow. The Fila-ment Group released a study (*https://www.filamentgroup.com/lab/mv-initial-load-times.html*) recently that says the average initial page load time for simple Angular 1.x apps on mobile devices is 3–4 seconds. It can be even worse for more complex apps. This is most often an issue for consumer-facing apps, especially those that are typically accessed on a mobile device, but can be a problem for any app. The goal of rendering on the server for this use case is to lower the users' perception of the initial page load time so that they see real content in under one second, regardless of device or connection speed. This goal is much easier to achieve consistently with server rendering than with client-side rendering.

SEO

The Google search crawler continues to get better at indexing client-side rendered content, and there likely will be a future where server rendering is not needed for SEO, but today consumer-facing apps that really care about their search ranking need server rendering. Why?

- First, the crawler isn't perfect (yet). There are a number of situations where the crawler may not index exactly what is rendered. This is often due to either JavaScript incapabilities or timing issues with async loading.

- With server rendering, the crawler can determine exactly how long it takes before the user sees content (i.e., the document complete event). This is not as easy on the client side (and, as mentioned in the previous use case, when it is measured, it is often much slower than server rendering).

- There is no success story out there for a client-side-only web app that beats server-rendered websites for competitive keyword searches (for example, think about any major purchase item like "flat screen tv" or "best sedan 2015").

Browser support

The downside of using more advanced web technologies like Web Components is that it is hard to keep support for older browsers. This is why Angular 2 doesn't officially support anything less than IE9. However, depending on the app being built, it may be possible to replace certain rich-client behaviors with server-side behaviors to support older browsers while letting app developers take advantage of the latest web platform. A couple of examples:

- The app is mostly informational and it is OK for users on older browsers to just see the information without any of the client side functionality. In this case, it may be all right to give legacy browser users a completely server-rendered website while evergreen browser users get the full client-side app.

- The app must support IE8. Most of the client-side web app functionality works, but there is one component that uses functionality not supported by IE8. For that one component, the app could potentially fetch the fully rendered partial HTML from the server.

Link preview
> Programs that show website previews for provided links rely on server rendering. Due to the complexity involved with capturing client-side rendered web pages, these programs will likely continue to rely on server rendering for the foreseeable future. The most well known examples involve social media platforms like Facebook, G+, or LinkedIn. Similar to the SEO use case, this is only relevant for consumer-facing apps.

The Web App Gap

The "Web App Gap" is a term I made up that represents the time between when a user makes a URL request and when the user has a functional visible web page in his browser. For most client-side web apps this means waiting for the server response, then downloading assets, initializing the client app framework, fetching data, and then finally painting to the screen. For many web applications, this gap ends up being 3–7 seconds or more. That is 3–7 seconds where the user is just sitting there looking at a blank screen, or maybe a spinner. And according to the Filament Group (*https://www.filamentgroup.com/lab/mv-initial-load-times.html*), "57% [of users] said they will abandon a page if its load time is 3 seconds or more."

Many people today are spoiled by the mobile native user experience. They don't care if it is a web or mobile app; they want the app instantly rendered and instantly functional. How can we do that with web apps? In other words, how can we eliminate the Web App Gap?

Well, there are four potential solutions:

Shorten the gap
> There are certainly many different types of performance optimizations, like minifying your client-side JavaScript or leveraging caching. The problem is that there are some things that are completely outside your control, such as network bandwidth, the power of the client device, etc.

Lazy loading
> In most cases, an initial client request results in a huge payload returned from the server. This initial payload includes many things that are not necessarily used in the initial view. If you could reduce the initial payload to only what is needed for the initial view, it would likely be very small and would load extremely fast. While this approach works, it is hard to set up. I have not seen anyone out there that has a library or framework to enable you to do this right out of the box effectively.

Service workers
> Addy Osmani recently presented the idea of using an application shell architecture (*http://addyosmani.com/blog/application-shell/*) where a service worker run-

ning inside the browser downloads and caches all resources so that subsequent visits to a particular URL will result in an application that is instantly rendered from the cache. The initial render, however, may still be slow as resources, download and not all browsers support service workers (see "Can I use...?" (*http://caniuse.com/#feat=serviceworkers*)).

Server rendering
The initial server response contains a fully rendered page that can be displayed to the user immediately. Then, as the user starts looking over the page and deciding what to do, the client app loads in the background. Once the client finishes initializing and getting any data that it needs, it takes over and controls everything from there.

This last solution is built into Angular 2, and you can get it for free.

Angular 2 Rendering Architecture

The Angular 2 server rendering architecture is laid out in Figure 13-2.

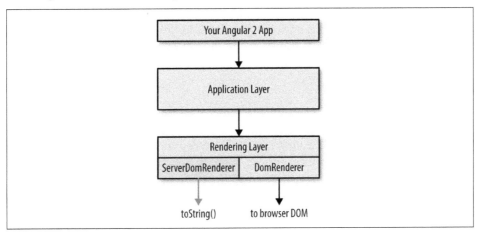

Figure 13-2. Angular 2 server rendering

Let's break this down:

Your Angular 2 app
At the top of the diagram is your custom code that you write on top of Angular 2. Your custom code interfaces with the Angular 2 application-layer API.

Application layer
The application layer has no dependencies on any specific environment. This means there is no direct reference to the window object or the browser object or the Node.js process object. Everything in the application layer can be run in the

browser or on the server or on a mobile device. This layer will run your components, make HTTP calls, and "compile" your app. The output of the compilation process is a component tree where each component contains two primary data objects: the bindings and something called a ProtoView, which is essentially an internal representation of a component template. The component tree is passed from the application layer to the rendering layer.

Rendering layer

There are two parts to the rendering layer. The first part is a common interface that is referenced by the application layer. That interface then defers to a specific `Renderer`. The default is the `DomRenderer`, which outputs to the browser DOM, but this can be easily overwritten through the Angular 2 Dependency Injector. For server rendering, we wrote the `ServerDomRenderer`, which outputs HTML to a string. The server-side bootstrap process sets the `ServerDomRenderer` instead of the `DomRenderer`.

The only caveat when you want your Angular 2 app to render on the server is that you can't directly reference any DOM objects in your code. For example, instead of using the global `window` object, you would use the `Window` class that is part of the Angular 2 API. This makes it easy for Angular 2 to limit the surface area of global client-side objects and provide some level of guarantee that equivalent functionality will exist on the server.

Preboot

Near the end of the presentation I threw in one more thing that we had just recently figured out. The approach we took improved perceived performance, but there was an issue. What happens to user events on the page between the time the user can see the server-rendered view and the time when the client takes over and has control? As we have talked about, that can sometimes be 2–6 seconds or more. During this time, the user can see something but may become frustrated as she attempts to interact with the page and nothing happens (or, worse, something unexpected happens). This is especially a problem with forms. For example, what happens when a user clicks a submit button on a server-rendered view before the client has control? And what happens if the user is in the process of typing in a text box during the switch from server to client view?

The most common solutions for this type of situation usually include:

1. Don't use server rendering for client-side forms.
2. Disable form elements until the client bootstrap is complete.

We didn't like either of these solutions, so we created a new library called Preboot that was designed to handle events in a server view before the client takes control. So, the user can type in a text box, click a button, or perform any other activity on a page and the client will seamlessly handle those events once the client-side bootstrap is complete. The user experience in most cases is that the page is instantly functional, which is exactly what we were trying to achieve.

And the best part is that this library is not Angular 2 specific. You can use this with Angular 1, and you can use it with React or Ember or any other framework. Pretty awesome stuff.

Angular Universal

The response to our AngularU talk was loud and emphatic. Developers loved the idea and wanted to use the feature as soon as possible. Brad and Tobias decided to turn our efforts into an official project under the Angular banner and call it Angular Universal (*https://github.com/angular/universal*).

Before we moved to this official Angular repo, much of what we did was completely outside the core Angular 2 libraries. Over the course of the following three months, we started to move several pieces into the core. By the time Angular 2 is released, we expect the Angular Universal library to be extremely thin and to mostly consist of integration libraries for specific backend Node.js frameworks like Express or Hapi.js.

Full-Stack Angular 2

Up to this point I have only talked about server rendering, but that is just one part of a much bigger concept: full-stack JavaScript development. Server rendering often gets the most focus because it can be the hardest challenge to overcome, but the real goal is using the same JavaScript everywhere for everything. It turns out that Angular 2 is an amazing framework to use for this purpose. Before we get to that, however, let me take a step back and explain why you should care about full-stack JavaScript development.

One piece of advice many of us have heard before is "use the right tool for the job." It sounds smart. And it is... to a degree. The problem is that the implementation of this idea doesn't always work out the way you might hope. Here are some of the issues we face:

Committees
  At many large organizations you can't just choose some new technology and start using it. You need to get it approved by three or four or five different committees (which is always fun). And when you do this, the decision may end up being more political than based on merit.

Contention

In some work environments, choosing a technology can cause a lot of tension among team members who have different options.

Context switching

Even if you don't have one of the first two issues, when you work in a diverse technical environment you run into problems with context switching. Either developers end up working on many different technologies, in which case there is some mental loss when they switch from one thing to another, or you split your teams along technical boundaries, in which case there is still some loss in productivity from the additional communication that is needed.

Code duplication

Finally, it is nearly impossible to avoid code duplication when you have a diverse technical environment. Typically there are things common throughout the organization, like security standards and data models, that need to be implemented within each language.

How many people do you think have run into one of these problems at work? There are many ways to solve or avoid these issues, but I have one simple solution: use a hammer and treat everything as a nail. Just pick one primary technology, and use that for nearly everything. If you can do that, all of these problems go away.

Of course, that sounds great in theory… but the reality is that for a long time there haven't been any great tools that are capable of being this magical hammer that can do everything. JavaScript is the only thing that runs everywhere, so if you want to try to use one technology for everything, it has to be JavaScript.

That is sort of weird to think about, given the fact that JavaScript used to be terrible in the browser, let alone on the server or in mobile devices. But it has been getting better and better over the years. It is now to the point where we are on the precipice of something amazing.

So yes, it is hard to fulfill the promise of full-stack development with vanilla ES5 Java-Script—but when you combine some of the features of ES6 and ES7 with Angular 2, you have all you need to start building amazing full-stack applications. Here are some of the features that help make full-stack development easy:

Universal dependency injection

Angular 1 DI was effective, but somewhat flawed. Angular 2 DI is absolutely amazing. Not only does it work on the client or the server, but it can be used outside Angular altogether. This makes it extremely easy to build a full-stack application because you can use DI to switch out any container-specific code (e.g., code tightly coupled to the browser that references the `window` object).

Universal server rendering
We discussed this earlier.

Universal event emitting
Angular 2 leverages RxJS observables for events. This works the same way on the client and the server. In Angular 1, event emitting was tied to the client-side `$scope`, which doesn't exist on the server.

Universal routing
Similar to event emitting, routing in Angular 2 works equally well on the client and the server.

ES6 modules
One module format to rule them all! Now you can author your JavaScript in one format that can be used everywhere.

ES7 decorators (TypeScript)
When doing large full-stack development, there are often cross-cutting concerns like security and caching that can be more easily implemented with custom decorators in TypeScript.

Tooling (Webpack, JSPM, Browserify)
All the new module bundlers are able to take one entry point and walk the dependency tree in order to generate one packaged JavaScript file. This is extremely helpful for full-stack development because it means you don't have to have separate */server* and */client* folders. Instead, all the client-side files are picked out through the dependency tree.

GetHuman.com

I mentioned earlier that I had created a server rendering solution in Angular 1 for GetHuman. At the time I am writing this chapter, this solution has been in production for over six months. So, was the promise of server rendering and full-stack development fulfilled?

I can say unequivocally and definitively, *yes*. Consider the following:

Performance
In many cases, users see the initial view in just over one second.

Scalability
We have been able to easily support 1,000+ simultaneous users with just three single-core web servers.

Productivity

Up until recently, we only had two full-time developers working on a dozen different web apps.

We continue to iterate and improve our Angular 1 infrastructure while at the same time prototyping what we will do with Angular 2. To that end, I have created an open source ecommerce app at FullStackAngular2.com (*http://fullstackangular2.com/*) where we hope to come up with an idiomatic way of building full-stack apps with Angular 2.

Postscript

To get more information about Angular Universal and building full-stack Angular 2 apps, check out the following links:

- Angular Universal code (*https://github.com/angular/universal*)
- Angular Universal examples (*https://github.com/angular/universal-starter*)
- Full Stack Angular 2 example (*http://fullstackangular2.com*)
- My blog (*https://medium.com/@jeffwhelpley*)
- Twitter (@jeffwhelpley (*https://twitter.com/jeffwhelpley*) and @gdi2290 (*https://twitter.com/gdi2290*))

CHAPTER 14

Brisket

Wayne Warner

Brisket is an isomorphic JavaScript framework built on top of Backbone.js. Brisket was developed by my team, the Consumer Web team at Bloomberg LP. It was published in Bloomberg's organization on GitHub on October 2, 2014 under the Apache 2 open source license.

My team engineered Brisket with three guiding principles:

- Code freedom
- Consistent API across environments
- Stay out of the way of progress

Before diving deeper into Brisket, why did we build it?

The Problem

Like most frameworks, Brisket was born out of a product need. In late 2013, my team was tasked with relaunching Bloomberg.com's opinion section as a new digital media product, BloombergView.com. The product team and designers had ambitious goals for the new site:

- Infinite scroll
- Pop-over lightboxed articles
- Responsive design (mobile first)
- Feels fast
- Great for SEO

We had 4 engineers and 3 months (12 weeks).

At the time, my team had only built traditional sites—server-side rendered pages with a mashup of client-side (in the browser) code to handle interactivity. A good example of a traditional website is IGN.com (*http://www.ign.com*). We used Ruby on Rails for our server-side rendering, and a combination of jQuery, some Backbone.js, and vanilla JavaScript for our client-side code. We built only traditional sites because they are great for quickly rendering pages on the server and provide strong SEO.

Fast page rendering is critical to a digital media product's success because media content is a fairly elastic product—if I can read the same thing somewhere else, but faster, that's where I'll go. Great SEO (a page that can be crawled and indexed by search engines) is also critical because search engines remain one of the highest drivers of traffic for digital media products.

Where traditional sites tend to come up short is when a site has a lot of client-side functionality. We anticipated the following problems with using the traditional site approach for the new site:

Unable to share templates or business logic
> The new site would require client-side rendering for features like infinite scroll and lightboxed articles. Since our server-side templates were written in Ruby, we could not reuse them on the client side. We would have to re-create them in JavaScript. Using two languages would also force us to maintain two sets of data models (a set for Ruby and a set for JavaScript) that did essentially the same thing.

Bad encapsulation for features
> With a traditional site, the server renders the markup for the feature, then the client-side code adds more functionality. It is more difficult to reason about the full lifecycle of a feature whose code is distributed across languages and (likely) folders in the filesystem.

Perceived slow navigation between pages
> Clicking to a new page in a traditional site often feels slow (even if it's actually not). Between the browser making a round-trip to the server for a new page, rerendering everything on the page, and rerunning any client-side code, the transition from page to page seems slower than it may actually be.

A single-page application, where the server renders minimal markup and a client-side application renders content and handles interactions, seemed a better fit for the new site. A good example of an SPA in the wild is Pandora. SPAs are great at keeping all of the application code together, providing faster perceived page transitions, and building rich user interfaces. However, an SPA was not a panacea. Drawbacks included:

Slow initial page load

Although SPAs feel fast while navigating within them, they usually have a slow initial page load. The slowness comes from downloading all of the application's assets and then starting the application. Until the application has started, the user cannot read any content.

No SEO

Since an SPA does not typically render markup on the server, it also does not produce any content for a search engine to crawl. In late 2013, search engines had begun attempting to crawl SPAs; however, that technology was too new (risky) for us to rely on.

Traditional sites and SPAs have complementary strengths; i.e., each one's strengths address the other's weaknesses. So the team asked, "How do we get all the goodness from both approaches?"

Best of Both Worlds

"Isomorphic JavaScript," a term popularized by Spike Brehm's article (*http:// nerds.airbnb.com/isomorphic-javascript-future-web-apps/*) on Airbnb's work on Rendr, describes JavaScript that can be shared between the client and the server. Rendr pioneered using the same code base to render pages through a Node.js server and handle client-side functionality with an SPA in the browser. Sharing a codebase this way is exactly what we wanted, but it came at the risk of potentially sacrificing our existing tools (i.e., Ruby, Rails, jQuery, etc.). Essentially, my team would be rebuilding all of our infrastructure. Before taking such a large risk, we explored a few options.

The first approach we considered was writing an SPA and using a headless browser to render pages on the server. But we ultimately decided that building two applications —an SPA and a headless browser server—was too complex and error-prone.

Next, the team explored the isomorphic frameworks that were available in late 2013. However, we didn't find a lot of stable offerings; most of the isomorphic frameworks were still very young. Of the frameworks that we considered, Rendr was one of the few that were running in production. Because it seemed the least risky, we decided to try Rendr.

We were able to build a working prototype of BloombergView using Rendr, but we wanted more flexibility in the following areas:

Templating

Rendr shipped with Handlebars templates by default; however, we preferred to use Mustache templates. Swapping Mustache for Handlebars did not seem like a straightforward task.

File organization

Like Rails, in some cases Rendr preferred convention over configuration. In other words, an application would only work correctly if its files followed a specific folder structure. For this project, we wanted to use a domain-driven folder structure (i.e., article, home page, search folders) rather than functionality-driven (i.e., views, controllers, models). The idea was to keep all things related to the article together so they would be easy to find.

Code style

Our biggest concern was how Rendr dictated our coding style for describing a page. As you can see in code in Example 14-1, Rendr controllers describe the data to fetch, but there's not much flexibility. It wasn't clear how to build a route if the data was a simple object rather than a model/collection. Also, since the controller did not have direct access to the View, we knew the View would be forced to handle responsibilities that we wanted to manage in our controllers.

Example 14-1. Rendr controller from 2013

```
var _ = require('underscore');

module.export = {
    index: function(params, callback) {
        var spec = {
            collection: {collection: 'Users', params: params}
        };
        this.app.fetch(spec, function(err, result){
            callback(err, result);
        });
    },
    show: function(params, callback) {
        var spec = {
            model: {model: 'User', params: param},
            repos: {collection: 'Repos', params: {user: params.login}}
        };
        this.app.fetch(spec, function(err, result){
            callback(err, result);
        });
    }
}
```

After exploring other solutions, we decided to try building the site from scratch.

Early Brisket

Having spent 2 of our 12 weeks exploring options, we wanted to save time by building on top of one of the major client-side JS frameworks—Backbone, Angular, or Ember.

All three had their merits, but we chose Backbone as our base because it was the easiest to get working on the server side.

Over the next 10 weeks we finished building the site. However, with such a tight timetable, there was no telling where the framework began and the application ended.

Making It Real

After a few months, my team was tasked with building a new application, Bloomberg-Politics.com, and rebuilding Bloomberg.com. The projects were to be built in two and three months respectively, without any downtime in between. With these tight timetables approaching, we took the opportunity to extract the tools from Bloomberg-View into a real framework—Brisket. Here are some of the key tools we were able to extract:

`Brisket.createServer`
> A function that returns an Express engine that you can use in your application to run a Brisket application

`Brisket.RouterBrewery`
> Brews routers that know how to route on the server and the client

`Brisket.Model`, `Brisket.Collection`
> Environment-agnostic implementations of the standard Backbone model and collection

`Brisket.View`
> Our version of a `Backbone.View` that allows support for some of the core features —reattaching Views, child View management, memory management, etc.

`Brisket.Templating.TemplateAdapter`
> Inherit from this to tell Brisket how to render templates

`Brisket request/response objects`
> Normalized request/response objects that provide tools like cookies, an application-level referrer, setting response status, etc.

All of these tools were extracted and refactored with Brisket's core principles—code freedom a consistent API across environments, and staying out of the way of progress —in mind.

Code Freedom

What we learned from Rendr is that using a complete isomorphic framework that includes modeling, routing, data fetching, and rendering is pretty difficult unless you reduce the scope of what developers can write. We knew Brisket could not provide the level of freedom that a regular Backbone application could, but we endeavored to get as close as possible.

The only requirement in a Brisket application is that you must return a View or a promise of a View from your route handlers. Everything else should feel as if you're writing an idiomatic Backbone application. Brisket takes on the responsibility of placing your View in the page rather than each route handler placing the View. Similar to a route handler in the Spring framework, your route handlers' job is to construct an object. Some other system in the framework is responsible for rendering that object.

Think of a route handler as a black box (as represented in each of the following figures). On the initial request, when the user enters a URL in the browser, Express handles the request. Express forwards the request to your application (the Backbone rendering engine). The input to the black box is a request, and the output is a single View. The ServerRenderer, the receiver of the View, has several jobs:

1. Serialize the View combined with the route's layout.
2. Send the result of all the data fetches (a.k.a. "bootstrapped data") made during the current server-side request with the HTML payload.
3. Render metatags.
4. Render the page title.
5. Set an HTML base tag that will make Brisket "application links" function correctly even without Brisket.

An application link is any anchor tag with a relative path. Application links are used to navigate to other routes in your application. All other types of links (e.g., absolute paths, fully qualified URLs, mailto links, etc.) function the same as in any other web page. By setting the base tag, you ensure that if JavaScript is disabled, or a user clicks an application link before the JavaScript has finished downloading, the browser will navigate to the expected path the old-fashioned way—a full page load of the new content. This way, the user can always access content. The initial page request process is illustrated in Figure 14-1.

Once the serialized View reaches the browser, your application picks up where it left off on the server. A good way to think about it is that the View reanimates with the same state that it had on the server. To reanimate the View, Brisket reruns the route that fired on the server. This time, though, rendering is handled by the ClientRenderer. The ClientRenderer knows which Views are already in the page and does not completely render them. Instead, as Views are initialized in the browser, if they already exist in the page, the ClientRenderer attaches them to the stringified versions of themselves.

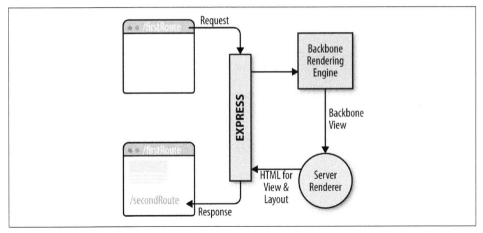

Figure 14-1. Initial page request

After the first route has completed, when the user clicks an application link, rather than heading all the way back to the server, the request is handled by the application in the browser. Your route handler works the same as it did on the server—it accepts a request, and returns a View. Your View is sent to the `ClientRenderer`, which updates the content in the layout. This is depicted in Figure 14-2.

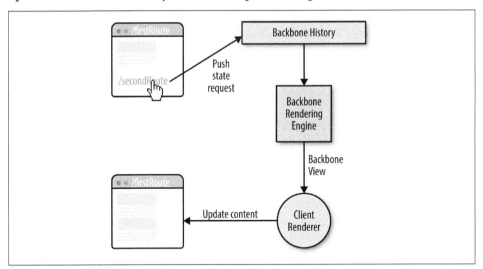

Figure 14-2. Subsequent "page" requests

Since your route handler receives the same input and is expected to produce the same output, you can write it without thinking about what environment it will run in. You can manage your code however you like in a route handler. Example 14-2 shows an example of a Brisket route handler.

Example 14-2. Brisket route handler

```
const RouterBrewery = require('path/to/app/RouterBrewery');
const Example = require('path/to/app/Example');
const ExampleView = require('path/to/app/ExampleView');

const ExampleRouter = RouterBrewery.create({
  routes: {
    'examples/:exampleId': 'example'
  },
  example: function(exampleId, layout, request, response) {
    if (!request.cookies.loggedIn) {
      response.redirect('/loginpage');
    }
    request.onComplete(function() {
      layout.doSomething();
    });
    const example = new Example({ exampleId });
    example.fetch()
      .then(() => {
        const exampleView = new ExampleView({ example });
        exampleView.on('custom:event', console.log);
        return exampleView;
      });
  }
});
```

This handler primarily chooses the View to render but also uses event bubbling, makes decisions based on cookies, and does some work when the route is visible to the user ("complete").

You may also notice that the objects required to construct the View must be entered in manually. Brisket opts for *your configuration* over our convention. You have the freedom to organize your application and create the conventions that make sense for you.

Use Any Templating Language

For our new applications, my team chose to use Hogan.js (a compiled flavor of Mustache). However, based on our work with Rendr, we wanted to keep the cost of switching templating engines as low as possible. By default, Brisket ships with a simple yet powerful (especially when used with ES6 template strings) `StringTem plateAdapter`, but, using inheritance, it can be overridden for either all your Views or a subset of them.

To switch templating engines for a View, inherit from `Brisket.Templating.Templa teAdapter` and implement `templateToHtml` to build a custom `TemplateAdapter`. Example 14-3 shows the implementation and usage of a simple Mustache template adapter.

Example 14-3. Simple Mustache template adapter

```
const MustacheTemplateAdapter = TemplateAdapter.extend({
    templateToHTML(template, data, partials) {
        return Mustache.render(template, data);
    }
});

const MustacheView = Brisket.View.extend({
    templateAdapter: MustacheTemplateAdapter
});
```

Changing a View's templating engine requires just a few lines of code. Any Views that inherit from this View will use its templating engine too.

Consistent API Across Environments

By providing a consistent API that is predictable in any environment, Brisket helps developers spend time focusing on their application's logic rather than on "what environment is my code running in?"

Model/Collection

Brisket provides environment-agnostic implementations of Backbone models and collections. From the developer's perspective, modeling with Brisket is the same as modeling with Backbone. On the client side, models fetch data using jQuery. On the server side, models also use jQuery. The server-side version of jQuery's Ajax transport is backed by the Node.js `http` package. Example 14-4 shows a sample Brisket model.

Example 14-4. Brisket model

```
const Side = Brisket.Model.extend({
    idAttribute: 'type',
    urlRoot: '/api/side',
    parse: function(data) {
        return data.side;
    }
});
```

Brisket used jQuery as the client-side transport because Backbone uses jQuery for fetching data by default. In order to maintain a consistent API between both environments, Brisket also uses jQuery on the server side to fetch data. For the server side, my team would have preferred to use Node.js-specific tools like `http` or `request`, but it was more important to maintain a consistent API between both environments.

Currently, we are working on dropping jQuery as the transport so that fetching data can be simpler and more powerful. On the client side, we are exploring using the new Fetch API. On the server side, we want to switch to http or request.

View Lifecycle

In order to keep its Views environment agnostic, Brisket hijacks their render method. When View.render is called, Brisket executes a rendering workflow:

1. Call the View's beforeRender callback.
2. Merge the View's model and any View logic specified by the View's logic function into a single data object.
3. Using the View's template adapter, template, and the data from step 1, render the template into the View's internal element.
4. Call the View's afterRender callback.

Use the beforeRender callback to set up data, queue up child views, and/or pick a template to use before Brisket renders the View's template. beforeRender is called on both the client AND the server.

Use the afterRender callback to modify your View after Brisket has rendered the View's template into the el. This is useful if you have to do some work (e.g., add a special class) that can only be done once the template has been rendered. afterRen der is called on both the client and the server.

Brisket Views also have a callback called onDOM. Once the View enters the page's DOM, use the onDOM callback to make changes to the View on the client side. The onDOM callback is a place where you can safely expect a window object to be available. So if you need to use a jQuery plugin that only works in a browser, for example, this is the place to do it. onDOM is called on the client but not the server.

During a View's rendering workflow, you can expect that beforeRender will always be called before afterRender. On the client, onDOM will be called only after afterRen der and when the View enters the page's DOM.

Aside from these Brisket-specific methods, you can manipulate a Brisket View as you would a Backbone view. To facilitate this level of flexibility, we use jsdom for server-side rendering. Most other isomorphic frameworks have shied away from using it for rendering because it is relatively slow and heavyweight for rendering server-side content. We saw the same thing, but chose to use it because the flexibility to code how we wanted outweighed the performance hit. We hope to replace jsdom with a server-side rendering implementation that only parses into the DOM as needed.

Child View Management

In a standard Backbone application, child view management can be tricky. While it is straightforward to render one view inside another, it is not as straightforward to manage the relationship between the views. Memory management is another pain point. A common problem with Backbone applications is causing memory leaks by forgetting to clean up views that are no longer visible to the user. In a browser, where a user sees only a few pages, a memory leak may not be catastrophic, but in an isomorphic environment your client-side memory leak is also a server-side memory leak. A big enough leak will take down your servers (as we learned the hard way).

Brisket provides a child View management system that helps you manage memory and display child Views. Brisket's child View handles all the bookkeeping for associating parent and child Views. It also makes sure to clean up Views as you navigate between routes, and the child View system comes with helpful methods to place a child View within the parent View's markup. The child View system works the same way in all environments.

Tools That Do What You Expect in All Environments

Along the way, while working on multiple consumer-facing projects using Brisket, we encountered several problems that would have been straightforward to handle in either a traditional application or an SPA but were tricky in an isomorphic application. Here are a few features in Brisket that were derived from solving these problems:

Redirecting to another URL

Brisket's `response` object provides a `redirect` method with the same signature as the `response` object of an Express engine. It does what you would expect—redirects to the new URL you provide with an optional status code. That's fine on the server, but in an isomorphic application, it's possible to navigate to a route that calls `response.redirect` in the browser. What should that do? Should it do a push-state navigation to another route in the application? Should it do nothing? Ultimately, we decided that calling `response.redirect` should trigger a full page load of the new page, like a redirect on the server would. Also, we made sure the new URL replaces the originally requested URL in the browser's history using `window.location.replace`.

Request referrer

In a traditional website, the request's referrer is available via `request.referrer` in an Express middleware or, on the client, in the browser's `document.referrer` property. In an SPA, `document.referrer` is correct on the initial page load, but not after you navigate to a new "page" within the application. We needed to solve this problem so that we could make accurate tracking calls for analytics. A normalized referrer is available via Brisket's `request.referrer` property.

Stay Out of the Way of Progress

Making Brisket extremely flexible has been critical to its high interoperability with third-party tools. We continue to look to the community for great solutions to common problems and do not want our framework to get in the way of that. By minimizing the rules around building a Brisket application, we've made sure there are ample places to integrate any third-party code even if it is not completely isomorphic.

ClientApp and ServerApp

My team started BloombergView with a strong knowledge base about jQuery plugins. After trying to use jQuery plugins, we quickly learned that they are not generally isomorphic-friendly—they only function correctly on the client side. Being able to use jQuery plugins and other client side-only code was the impetus for creating the `ClientApp` and `ServerApp` classes.

Brisket provides a base `ClientApp` and `ServerApp` that you can inherit from. Your implementations act as environment-specific initializers. These classes are a great place to set up environment-specific logging, initialize jQuery plugins, or enable/disable functionality depending on the environment.

Layout Template

Brisket provides a `Layout` class that inherits from `Brisket.View`. The layout's template is where you define the `<html>`, `<head>`, and `<body>` tags of your pages. Brisket allows you to use different layouts for each router. Currently, using multiple layouts only works on the server side because of the complexity of swapping layouts in the browser. Since the layout template is just standard markup like any other template, it's a good place to put third-party embedded code for common requirements such as ads, tracking pixels, etc.

Other Lessons Learned

Brisket has been great for my team. We have been able to hit (or just narrowly miss) our extremely tight deadlines and produce great digital products with it. Although these sites have been successful, we've learned a lot of lessons along the way. Here are a few:

Avoid monolithic client-side bundles
> A general problem for SPAs has always been large CSS and JS bundles. As applications grow and code bundles grow, the initial page load gets slower. We are working on new features in Brisket to make it easier to split up the application bundle.

Prevent memory leaks

When writing an SPA, sometimes you forget your code runs on a server. Using singletons or not cleaning up event bindings can lead to memory leaks. Closing resources is a general good practice that many frontend developers did not have to pay attention to before the advent of SPAs. In SPAs and especially isomorphic applications, good coding practices must be followed.

Building your own framework can be frustrating

Although it was exciting to build our own framework, with our tight deadlines it was frustrating when it was impossible to execute on a feature because Brisket did not have the tools yet. On the positive side, each moment of frustration led to a great new addition to (or subtraction from) Brisket.

What's Next for Brisket?

My team currently uses Brisket in production on multiple consumer-facing products, including our flagship Bloomberg.com. We continue to evolve Brisket so that our users have a better experience and so that developing with it continues to be enjoyable and productive. Despite powering several large-scale sites in production, Brisket is still a sub-1.0.0 project. As of this writing, we are actively working toward a 1.0.0 release. Some of the new features/improvements we have in mind are:

- Make it easier to split up a large Brisket application into smaller bundles.
- Rearchitect server-side rendering for speed.
- Continue to simplify and refine the API.
- Decouple from jQuery.
- Future-proof for the arrival of generators, async functions, and template strings.

While Brisket has served us well so far, we continue to experiment with new technologies and approaches for building our products. Our team is not locked into any technology, even Brisket. We always want to use the best technology to solve our product needs, regardless of the source.

Postscript

Building Brisket has been quite a journey, full of ups and downs. To learn more about Brisket and keep up to date with the project, check us out on npm (*https://www.npmjs.com/package/brisket*). Also try out the Brisket generator (*https://www.npmjs.com/package/generator-brisket*).

CHAPTER 15

"Colony" Case Study: Isomorphic Apps Without Node

Patrick Kunka, Richard Davis, and Andrew Barker

Colony is a global film-streaming platform connecting content owners with passionate fans through exclusive extra content. In a landscape of significant competition, our go-to-market strategy relies heavily on a world-class product and user experience, with ambitions to redefine the way film is consumed online.

The Problem

An important differentiation between Colony's video-on-demand model and that of competitors like Netflix is our transactional business model: content on our platform is open to the public to browse and purchase on a pay-as-you-go basis, and isn't hidden behind a subscription paywall. We benefit from letting Google crawl and index our entire catalogue as a result. On top of this, the nature of our product requires a dynamic user interface that must frequently update to reflect changes to a complex application state. For example, elements must update to reflect whether the user is signed in or not, and whether the content bundle (or parts of it) is owned or at a certain point in its rental period. While our initial prototype was built using out-of-the-box ASP.NET MVC, we soon realized that turning our frontend into a single-page app would vastly improve our ability to deal with these challenges, while also enabling our backend and frontend teams to work independently of one another by "decoupling" the stack.

We were therefore faced with the dilemma of how to combine a traditional server-rendered and indexable website with a single-page app. At the time in 2014, isomorphic frameworks like Meteor provided this sort of functionality out of the box but required a Node.js backend. SPA frameworks like Angular and Ember also were already ubiquitous, but they came hand-in-hand with SEO drawbacks that we wanted to avoid.

Our backend had already been built in ASP.NET MVC, and two-thirds of our development team was made up of C# developers. We wondered if there was a way we could achieve something similar to an isomorphic application, but without a Node.js backend and without having to rebuild our entire application from scratch. How could C# and JavaScript—technologies that are typically viewed as separate and incompatible—be brought together? In other words, could we build an isomorphic application without Node.js?

Solving this problem would also provide us with numerous performance benefits and the ability to instantly render the application in very specific states—for example, linking to a film page with its trailer open, or rendering the checkout journey at a specific point. As most of this UI takes place within "modals" in our design, these are things that would traditionally be rendered by JavaScript and could be managed only in the frontend.

We wanted the ability to server render any page or view in any particular state based on its URL, and then have a client-side JavaScript application start up in the background to take over the rendering and routing from that point on. For this to happen we would firstly need a common templating language and shared templates. Secondly, we would need a common data structure for expressing the application state.

Up until this point, view models had been the responsibility of the backend team, but with an ideal decoupled stack, all view design and templating would be the responsibility of the frontend team, including the structure and naming of the data delivered to the templates.

From the perspective of removing any potential duplication of effort or code, we pondered the following questions:

1. Was there a templating language with implementations in both C# and JavaScript? For this to be conceivable, it would need to be "logicless," and therefore not allow any application code in the templates in the way that C# Razor or PHP does.

2. If a component was needed by both the frontend and the backend, could it be expressed in a language-agnostic data format such as JSON?

3. Could we write something (for instance, a view model) in one language and automatically transpile it to another?

Templating

We began by looking at templating. We were big fans of Handlebars, due to its strict logicless nature and its intentionally limited scope. Given a template, and a data object of any structure, Handlebars will output a rendered string. As it is not a full-blown view engine, it can be used to render small snippets, or integrated into larger frameworks to render an entire application. Its logicless philosophy restricts template logic to `#if`, `#unless`, and `#each`, the idea being that if anything more complex is needed, the template is not the place for it.

Although originally written for JavaScript, Handlebars can be used with any language for which an implementation exists, and as a result, implementations now exist for almost every popular server-side programming language. Thankfully for us, a well-maintained open source implementation for C# existed in the form of the excellent Handlebars.Net.

Our frontend had been built with a modular or "atomic" design philosophy, meaning that rather than using monolithic page templates, any particular view was made up from a sequence of reusable "modules" that could in theory function in any order or context. With our previous server-side view rendering solution in Razor, this concept didn't translate well from the frontend to the backend, as our backend team would need to take the static modules, stitch them together into larger constructs, and insert the necessary logic and template tags as desired. With a shared templating language and data structure, however, there was no reason why we couldn't now share these individual modules between both sides of the stack and render them in the desired order using either C# or JavaScript, with identical results. The process of designing a module, templating it, and making it dynamic could then be done entirely by the frontend team.

Data

One issue with our previous solution was the ad hoc nature of the view models in our prototype, which evolved organically per template as features were added. There was never a big picture of the overall application data structure, with data often being exposed to some templates and not others, requiring effort and care from both teams when creating new templates.

To avoid this problem early on, we designed a "global" data structure for the whole application that could represent the site, a resource, and the application state in a single object. On the backend, this structured data would be mapped from the database and delivered to Handlebars to render a view. On the frontend, the data would first be received over a REST API and then delivered to Handlebars. In each case, however, the final data provided to Handlebars would be identical.

The data structure we decided on was as follows. This object can be thought of as a state container for the entire application at any point in time:

```
{
  Site: {...},
  Entry: {...},
  User: {...},
  ViewState: {...},
  Module: {...}
}
```

The Site object holds data pertaining to the entire website or application, irrespective of the resource that's being viewed. Things like static text, Google Analytics ID, and any feature and environment toggles are contained here.

The Entry object holds data pertaining to the current resource being viewed (e.g., a page or a particular film). As a user navigates around the site, the requested resource's data is pulled in from a specific endpoint, and the entry property is updated as needed:

```
<head>
...
  <title>

    |


  </title>
</head>
```

The User object holds nonsensitive data pertaining to the signed-in user, such as name, avatar, and email address:

```
<aside class="user-sidebar">
  <h3>Hello !</h4>

      <h4>Your Recent Purchases</h4>


      ...


  </aside>
```

The ViewState object is used to reflect the current rendered state of a view, which is crucial to our ability to render complex states on the backend via a URL. For example, a single view can be rendered with a particular tab selected, a modal open, or an accordion expanded, as long as that state has its own URL:

```
<nav class="bundle-nav">
  <a href="/extras/" class="tab tab__active">Extras</a>
  <a href="/about/" class="tab tab__active">About</a>
</nav>
```

The `Module` object is not global, but is used when data must be delivered to a specific module without exposing it to other modules. For example, we may need to iterate through a list of items within an entry (say, a gallery of images), rendering an image module for each one, but with different data. Rather than that module having to pull its data out of the entry using its index as a key, the necessary data can be delivered directly to it via the `Module` object:

```
<figure class="image">
    <img src="" alt=""/>

        <figcaption>
            <p></p>
        </figcaption>

</figure>
```

Transpiled View Models

With our top-level data structure defined, the internal structure of each of these objects now needed to be defined. With C# being the strictly typed language that it is, arbitrarily passing dynamic object literals around in the typically loose JavaScript style would not cut it. Each view model would need strictly defined properties with their respective types. As we wanted to keep view model design the responsibility of the frontend, we decided that these should be written in JavaScript. This would also allow frontend team members to easily test the rendering of templates (for example, using a simple Express development app) without needing to integrate them with the .NET backend.

JavaScript constructor functions could be used to define the structure of a class-like object, with default values used to infer type.

Here's an example of a typical JavaScript view model in our application describing a `Bundle` and inheriting from another model called `Product`:

```
var Bundle = function() {
    Product.apply(this);
    this.Title      = '';
    this.Director   = '';
    this.Synopsis   = '';
    this.Artwork    = new Image();
    this.Trailer    = new Video();
    this.Film       = new Video();
    this.Extras     = [new Extra()];
    this.IsNew      = false;
};
```

Templates often require the checking of multiple pieces of data before showing or hiding a particular element. To keep templates clean, however, `#if` statements in

Handlebars may only evaluate a single property, and comparisons are not allowed without custom helper functions, which in our case would have to be duplicated. While more complex logic can be achieved by nesting logical statements, this creates unreadable and unmaintainable templates, and is against the philosophy of logicless templating. We needed to decide where the additional logic needed in these situations would live.

Thanks to the addition of "getters" in ES5 JavaScript, we were able to easily add dynamically evaluated properties to our constructors that could be used in our templates, which proved to be the perfect place to perform more complex evaluations and comparisons.

The following is an example of a dynamic ES5 `getter` property on a view model, evaluating two other properties from the same model:

```
var Bundle = function() {
    ...
    this.Trailer    = new Video();
    this.IsNew      = false;
    ...
    Object.defineProperty(this, 'HasWatchTrailerBadge', {
        get: function() {
            return this.IsNew && this.Trailer !== null;
        }
    });
};
```

We now had all of our view models defined with typed properties and getters, but the problem remained that they existed only in JavaScript. Our first approach was to manually rewrite each of them in C#, but we soon realized that this was a duplication of effort and was not scalable. We felt like we could automate this process if only we had the right tools. Could we somehow "transpile" our JavaScript constructors into C# classes?

We decided to try our hand at creating a simple Node.js app to do just this. Using enumeration, type checking, and prototypal inheritance we were able to create descriptive "manifests" for each of our constructors. These manifests contained information such as the name of the class and what classes, if any, it inherited from. At the property level, they contained the names and types of all properties, whether or not they were getters, and if so, what the getter should evaluate and what type it should return.

With each view model parsed into a manifest, the data could now be fed into (ironically) a Handlebars template of a C# class, resulting in a collection of production-ready *.cs* files for the backend, each describing a specific view model.

Here's the same `Bundle` view model, transpiled into C#:

```
namespace Colony.Website.Models
{
    public class Bundle : Product
    {
        public string Title { get; set; }
        public string Director { get; set; }
        public string Synopsis { get; set; }
        public Image Artwork { get; set }
        public Video Trailer { get; set; }
        public Video Film { get; set; }
        public List<Extra> Extras { get; set; }
        public Boolean IsNew { get; set; }
        public bool HasWatchTrailerBadge
        {
            get
            {
                return this.Is New && this.Trailer != null;
            }
        }
    }
}
```

It's worth noting that our transpiler is limited in its functionality—it simply converts a JavaScript constructor into a C# class. It cannot for example, take any piece of arbitrary JavaScript and convert it to the equivalent C#, which would be an infinitely more complex task.

Layouts

We now needed a way of defining which modules should be rendered for a particular view, and in what order.

If this became the responsibility of our view controllers, this list of modules and any accompanying logic would need to be duplicated in both C# and JavaScript. To avoid this duplication, we wondered if we could express each view as a JSON file (like the following simple example describing a possible layout of a home page) that again could be shared between the frontend and backend:

```
[
    "Head",
    "Header",
    "Welcome",
    "FilmCollection",
    "SignUpCta",
    "Footer",
    "Foot"
]
```

While listing the names of modules in a particular order was simple, we wanted the ability to conditionally render modules only when specific conditions were met. For example, a user sidebar should only be rendered if a user is signed in.

Taking inspiration from Handlebars's limited set of available logic (#if, #unless, #each), we realized we could express everything we needed to in JSON by referring to properties within the aforementioned global data structure:

```
[
    ...
    {
        "Name": "UserSidebar",
        "If": ["User.IsSignedIn"]
    },
    {
        "Name": "Modal",
        "If": ["ViewState.IsTrailerOpen"],
        "Import": "Entry.Trailer"
    }
]
```

Having restructured the format of the layout, we now had the ability to express simple logic and import arbitrary data into modules. Note that If statements take the form of arrays to allow the evaluation of multiple properties.

Taking things further, we began to use this format to describe more complex view structures where modules could be nested within other modules:

```
[
    ...
    {
        "Name": "TabsNav",
        "Unless": ["Entry.UserAccess.IsLocked"]
    },
    {
        "Name": "TabContainer",
        "Unless": ["Entry.UserAccess.IsLocked"]
        "Modules": [
            {
                "Name": "ExploreTab",
                "If": ["ViewState.IsExploreTabActive"],
                "Modules": [
                    {
                        "Name": "Extra",
                        "ForEach": "Entry.Extras"
                    }
                ]
            },
            {
                "Name": "AboutTab",
                "If": ["ViewState.IsAboutTabActive"]
            }
```

```
            ]
        }
        ...
    ]
```

The ability to express the nesting of modules allowed for complete freedom in the structuring of markup.

We had now arrived at a powerful format for describing the layout and structure of our views, with a considerable amount of logic available. Had this logic been written in either JavaScript or C#, it would have required tedious and error-prone manual duplication.

Page Maker

To arrive at our final rendered HTML on either side of the stack, we now needed to take our templates, layouts, and data and combine them all together to produce a view.

This was a piece of functionality that we all agreed would need to be duplicated, and would need to exist in both a C# and a JavaScript form. We designed a specification for a class that we called the "Page Maker," which would need to iterate through a given layout file, render out each module with its respective data as per the conditions in the layout file, and finally return a rendered HTML string.

As we needed to pay close attention to making sure that both implementations would return identical output, we wrote both the C# and JavaScript Page Makers as group programming exercises involving the whole development team, which also provided a great learning opportunity for frontend and backend team members to learn about each other's technology.

Frontend Single-Page App

Our development team culture had always been to build as much as we could in-house, and own our technology as a result. When it came to our single-page app, we had the choice of using an off-the-shelf framework like Angular, Backbone, or Ember, or building our own. With our templating taken care of, and our global data structure over the API effectively forming our application state, we still needed a few more components to manage routing, data binding, and user interfaces. We strongly believed, and still do, in the concept of "unobtrusive" JavaScript, so the blurring of HTML and JavaScript in Angular (and now React's JSX) was something we wanted to avoid. We also realized that trying to retrofit an opinionated framework onto our now quite unique architecture would result in significant hacking and a fair amount of redundancy in the framework. We therefore decided to build our own solution, with a few distinct principles in mind: firstly, UI behavior should not be tightly coupled to specific markup, and secondly, the combination of changes to the application state and the Handlebars logic already defined in our templates and layouts should be enough to enable dynamic rerendering of any element on the page at any time.

The solution we arrived at is not only extremely lightweight, but also extremely modular. At the lowest level we have our state and fully rendered views delivered from the server, where we can denote arbitrary pieces of markup to "subscribe" to changes in the state. These changes are signaled using DOM events, which we found to be much more performant than an Angular-like digest loop, or various experimental "Observable" implementations. When a change happens, that section of the DOM is rerendered and replaced. We were reassured to learn recently that the basic concept behind this is almost identical to that of the increasingly popular Redux library.

A level up, our user interface "behaviors" are entirely separate from this process, effectively progressively enhancing arbitrary pieces of markup. For example, we could apply the same "slider" UI behavior to a variety of different components, each with entirely different markup—in one case a list of films, in another case a list of press quotes.

At the highest level, a History API–enabled router was built to intercept all link clicks and determine which layout file was needed to render the resulting view. With the data forming our application state already delivered over a REST API from the server, we decided to expand this API to also deliver module templates and JSON layouts. This would ensure that these various shared resources could only ever exist in one place (the server), and thus reduce the risk of any divergence between the frontend and backend resources.

Final Architecture

The schematic in Figure 15-1 illustrates the full lifecycle of both the initial server-side request and all subsequent client-side requests, with the components used for each.

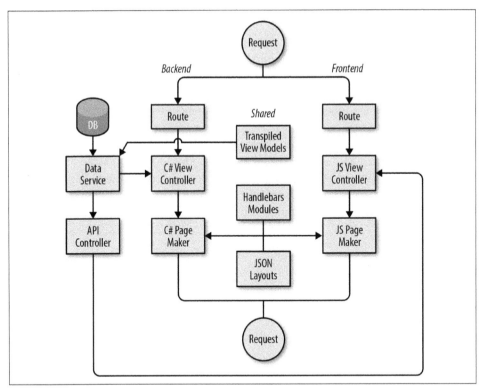

Figure 15-1. Lifecycle of initial server-side request and subsequent client-side requests

Next Steps

While sharing these various components heavily reduced code duplication in our application, there are areas where duplication still exists, such as our controllers and routes. Building upon what we learned from our layout files, however, there's no reason why our routes and parts of their respective controllers couldn't also be expressed as shared JSON files, and then fed into lightweight parsers with implementations in C# and JavaScript.

While several solutions have now started to arise allowing the rendering of Angular applications and React components on non-JavaScript engines (such as ReactJS.NET and React-PHP-V8JS), our solution is still unique in the ASP.NET ecosystem due to its lack of dependency on a particular framework. While our backend team did have to write some additional code (such as the Page Maker) during the development of the solution, their data services, controllers, and application logic were left more or less untouched. The amount of frontend UI code they were able to remove from the backend as a result of decoupling has led to a leaner backend application with a clearer purpose. While our application is in one sense "isomorphic," it is also cleanly divided, with a clear separation of concerns.

We imagine that there are many other development teams out there that, like us, desire the benefits of an isomorphic application but feel restrained by their choice of backend technology—whether that be C#, Java, Ruby, or PHP. In these cases, decisions made during the infancy of a company are now most likely deeply ingrained in the product architecture, and have influenced the structure of the development team. Our solution shows that isomorphic principles can be applied to any stack, without having to introduce a dependency on a frontend framework that may be obsolete in a year's time, and without having to rebuild an application from scratch. We hope other teams take inspiration from the lessons we've learned, and we look forward to seeing isomorphic applications across a range of technologies in the future.

CHAPTER 16

Final Thoughts

Charlie Robbins

I do not know what I may appear to the world, but to myself I seem to have been only like a boy playing on the sea-shore, and diverting myself in now and then finding a smoother pebble or a prettier shell than ordinary, whilst the great ocean of truth lay all undiscovered before me.

—Isaac Newton

In October 2009, I had never written JavaScript professionally. In fact, I had barely spent more than a few hours playing with the language. At the time I was writing frontend trading systems and other bank software in WPF (Windows Presentation Foundation), a technology I had been involved with at Microsoft. If you had told me that "isomorphic JavaScript" would become this widespread a concept before my original writing on the topic, I surely would have laughed. I want to highlight these facts to remind you that you really don't know what is possible until you try.

Families of Design Patterns, Flux, and Isomorphic JavaScript

Isomorphic JavaScript was not the main topic of my original blog post on the subject, "Scaling Isomorphic Javascript Code." (*https://blog.nodejitsu.com/scaling-isomorphic-javascript-code/*) The term was just a footnote to contextualize and justify what I thought was a much more impactful software design pattern at the time. The way that developers have adopted the term and abstract concept far more than any concrete software design pattern is fascinating.

Software design patterns evolve in a somewhat similar way to religions: there are multiple interpretations of the core ideas for each pattern, which can lead to vastly different characteristics in each sect. Of course, in the case of software design patterns a sect is really just another concrete implementation of the pattern. I will refer to this principle as the "family of design patterns" principle. Consider arguably the most popular design pattern of all time: MVC (Model–View–Controller). The original implementations of the MVC pattern in SmallTalk at the Xerox Palo Alto Research Center (PARC) bear little resemblance to the Model2-like MVC implementations in Ruby on Rails today. These differences mainly arose because Ruby on Rails is a server-based framework and the original MVC implementations focused on frontend desktop GUIs.

In the face of increasingly isomorphic JavaScript, the design patterns and software architectures needed to evolve. Practically speaking, this shift toward isomorphic JavaScript and one-way immutable data flow has validated the "family of design patterns" principle through the emergence of the Flux family of patterns. Flux has given rise to a plethora of implementations, most of which are isomorphic. The popularity of implementations has correlated with their capacity to support both client-side and server-side rendering. The rise of React, Flux, and popular implementations like Redux has validated the importance of isomorphic JavaScript. Indeed, the author of Redux has his own thoughts on the subject (*http://bit.ly/universaljs*).

Always Bet on JavaScript

Since October 2011, when I first mentioned isomorphic JavaScript, there is simply more JavaScript everywhere. If we use the total number of npm modules as a proxy for growth, then there was a over a *50x increase* in JavaScript between late 2011 and mid-2016. That is simply a staggering number when looking back on it, and what's even more staggering is that the growth of JavaScript shows no signs of slowing down.

The iconic phrase "always bet on JavaScript" used by JavaScript's creator, Brendan Eich, could never be more true than it is now. JavaScript is nearly everywhere today, powering dozens of different platforms, devices, and end uses. It runs on phones, drones, and automobiles and it tracks space suits at NASA while powering the text editor I'm using to write this.

Even more drastic than the growth in JavaScript adoption is the degree to which development of JavaScript has changed. In 2011 the first JS-to-JS compiler (or transpiler), Traceur, was released by Alex Russell at JSConf (*https://www.youtube.com/watch?v=ntDZa7ekFEA&t=1m42s*) as "a tool that's got an expiration date on it." Traceur and other JavaScript tooling like npm, browserify, and webpack have made transpilation widely available and much more accessible than ever before. This coincided with the finalization of the ES6/ES2015 specification.

These factors combined to make way for the cornerstone of modern JavaScript development: that is, the idea of *always and easily* running a transpiler like babel against your JavaScript before execution in the browser and adopting ES201{5,6,7...} features in a rapid, piecemeal way.

Certainly "always" couldn't exist without " easily," and getting to easily was an evolution. The adoption of npm as a workflow tool made managing JavaScript language tooling easier. Easier-to-use language tooling made the idea of always using a transpiler less abhorrent when it became absolutely necessary in frameworks with custom-syntax react and JSX.

This created an incredibly friendly environment for isomorphic JavaScript. Consider a scenario where a library doesn't perfectly fit into the environment or semantics you are working with for your application. Before this ubiquitous toolchain that would have prohibited you from using the library in question, but now your transpilation and bundling toolchain usually makes using that library possible.

There are exciting things on the horizon as well. WebAssembly (or wasm) is a new portable, size- and load-time-efficient format suitable for compilation to the Web. It creates a viable compilation target for many languages, and more importantly, well established-projects in those languages. The promise of WebAssembly goes beyond isomorphic JavaScript to seemingly endless possibilities for isomorphic code in general.

On Nomenclature and Understanding

Lastly, I'd like to discuss a few questions that I often get asked by developers. The first question is: "Why make up a new term for something so seemingly obvious as running the same code on a client and a server?" The answer I give is simple: because there wasn't a term for it yet. I also get asked, "Why base it on mathematics?" While I know my answer is contentious to some, it was obvious to me: because frontend build systems and, more recently, transpilers represent what I believe is an "isomorphism" in this sense of the word:

> iso•mor•phic (adj.)
> 1)
> a: being of identical or similar form, shape, or structure
> b: having sporophytic and gametophytic generations alike in size and shape
> **2) related by an *isomorphism***

More recently, and much more frequently, I find myself asked about the debate between "isomorphic JavaScript" and "universal JavaScript." Approaching this objectively, let's again consider *isomorphic JavaScript as a spectrum* and the *different categories of isomorphic JavaScript* (Chapters 2 and 3). The spectrum illustrates the range in complexity when working with and building isomorphic JavaScript. The three categories of isomorphic JavaScript demonstrate the degree to which one must adapt JavaScript based on complexity and environment:

- JavaScript that is *environment agnostic* runs "universally" with no modifications.
- JavaScript that is *shimmed for each environment* only runs in different environments if the environment itself is modified.

- JavaScript that uses *shimmed semantics* may require modifications to the environment or behave slightly differently between environments.

If "universal JavaScript" is that which requires no modifications to the code or the environment to be isomorphic, then *environment-agnostic* JavaScript is clearly universal. Therefore, as more changes are needed to either the code itself or the environments in which it runs, the code ceases to be universal and is more isomorphic (Figure 16-1).

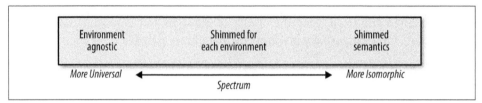

Figure 16-1. Universal and isomorphic JavaScript spectrum

When we consider the spectrum and categories together, the question "Is this isomorphic JavaScript or universal JavaScript?" becomes "Is this JavaScript more isomorphic or more universal?" This interpretation is vastly more technical and nuanced than my original definition for isomorphic JavaScript:

> By isomorphic we mean that any given line of code (with notable exceptions) can execute both on the client and the server.

It also illustrates a key point: the debate about and interpretation of these terms is endless and largely unimportant. For example, to the horror of JavaScript developers everywhere, I could point out that an automorphism is "an isomorphism whose source and target coincide." With this knowledge we could interpret "automorphic JavaScript" as another term for "universal JavaScript" since the code is identical in all environments. This new term would add no practical value to the shared understanding of the subject and only further cloud an otherwise simple (albeit nuanced) idea.

At this point you may be asking yourself, "Aren't technical nuances important to us developers?" While there certainly is no shortage of technical nuance in software, a technical argument about a new or different term to use should not be your focus as a developer. Your focus should be on using whatever understanding you may have (right or wrong) to do something you find interesting or innovative. Our shared understanding of all things, including JavaScript, is constantly changing. All castles made of code will eventually be obsolete, and I for one am looking forward to watching them crash into the sea.

Index

T

technical debt, Ajax and, xi
templates, 17, 47-49
templating engines, Brisket, 160
templatization, component, 133-136
Time to First Byte (TTFB), 131
tools, choosing, 149
Traceur, 180
transpiler/transpiling, 171-173, 180
Twitter, 3

U

universal JavaScript, 19, 181
URLs, redirects and (see redirects)
user requests (see requests, responding to)

V

view layer
    shared, 15-17
    sharing templates, 17
    sharing view logic, 17
view models, 171-173
virtual DOM, 129

W

Walmart.com
    delivery problems, 122
    importance of page load speed for, 1
    performance improvements, 136-139
    React.js and, 121-123, 130-139
        (see also React.js)
    TTFB problems, 131
WalmartLabs, ix, 121-123
wasm (WebAssembly), 181
Web App Gap, 146
WebAssembly, 181
Webpack, 68

X

XMLHttpRequest object, 7

About the Authors

Jason Strimpel is a staff software engineer on the Platform team at WalmartLabs who specializes in the UI layer. Jason has been building web applications for the past 12 years. Approximately three years ago he began specializing in the frontend—in particular, JavaScript—and since then he has worked with several component libraries and frameworks. However, Jason found limitations to these libraries when presented with uniquely challenging UI requirements, so he began developing his own custom components and catalog of helpers. He is an extremely passionate developer with a very bad sense of humor who loves simplifying the complexities that arise when building rich UIs.

Maxime Najim is a Software Architect and a full stack web developer. He has worked for companies like Yahoo!, Apple, and Netflix, creating large, highly scalable, and reliable web applications. He is currently focused on designing and implementing new systems and frameworks for Walmart's global ecommerce platform.

Colophon

The animal on the cover of *Building Isomorphic JavaScript Apps* is the gray tree frog (*Hyla versicolor*), a small frog native to eastern and central North America. The gray tree frog is so named for its arboreal habitat and gray coloring. However, as its scientific name would suggest, the gray tree frog has the ability to change its color from gray to green, much like a chameleon. This ability is used as camouflage to evade predators.

The gray tree frog can be found in forested regions as far south as Texas and as far north as New Brunswick. They rarely venture from their treetop homes except to breed. Gray tree frogs grow to about two inches in length and have lumpy skin like a toad (hence their nickname, the changeable toad). Their diet consists of a variety of insects, such as crickets, grasshoppers, and ants.

There are no major threats to the gray tree frog, and their population is believed to be stable. Gray tree frogs are sometimes kept as pets and live five to ten years.

Many of the animals on O'Reilly covers are endangered; all of them are important to the world. To learn more about how you can help, go to *animals.oreilly.com*.

The cover image is from *Wood's Illustrated Natural History*. The cover fonts are URW Typewriter and Guardian Sans. The text font is Adobe Minion Pro; the heading font is Adobe Myriad Condensed; and the code font is Dalton Maag's Ubuntu Mono.

Have it your way.

Get even more for your money.

Join the O'Reilly Community, and register the O'Reilly books you own. It's free, and you'll get:

- $4.99 ebook upgrade offer
- 40% upgrade offer on O'Reilly print books
- Membership discounts on books and events
- Free lifetime updates to ebooks and videos
- Multiple ebook formats, DRM FREE
- Participation in the O'Reilly community
- Newsletters
- Account management
- 100% Satisfaction Guarantee

Signing up is easy:

1. Go to: oreilly.com/go/register
2. Create an O'Reilly login.
3. Provide your address.
4. Register your books.

Note: English-language books only

To order books online:
oreilly.com/store

For questions about products or an order:
orders@oreilly.com

To sign up to get topic-specific email announcements and/or news about upcoming books, conferences, special offers, and new technologies:
elists@oreilly.com

For technical questions about book content:
booktech@oreilly.com

To submit new book proposals to our editors:
proposals@oreilly.com

O'Reilly books are available in multiple DRM-free ebook formats. For more information:
oreilly.com/ebooks

Milton Keynes UK
Ingram Content Group UK Ltd.
UKHW050029091024
449443UK00007B/147

9 781491 932933